Tibet

Tibet

BY PATRICIA KUMMER

Enchantment of the World
Second Series

Children's Press®

A Division of Scholastic Inc.

NEW YORK   TORONTO   LONDON   AUCKLAND   SYDNEY
MEXICO CITY   NEW DELHI   HONG KONG
DANBURY, CONNECTICUT

Frontispiece: Monks at Nechung monastery

Consultant: Kevin A. Vose, University of Virginia, Department of Religious Studies, Charlottesville

Please note: All statistics are as up-to-date as possible at the time of publication.

Book production by Herman Adler Design

Library of Congress Cataloging-in-Publication Data

Kummer, Patricia K.
  Tibet / by Patricia K. Kummer
    p. cm. — (Enchantment of the world. Second series)
Includes bibliographical references and index.
  ISBN 0-516-22693-2
  1. Tibet (China)—Juvenile literature. [1. Tibet (China)] I. Title. II. Series.
DS786.K495 2003
951'.5—dc21   2002156704

Acknowledgments

I wish to thank the staffs of the International Campaign for Tibet, the Office of Tibet, the Embassy of the People's Republic of China, and the Web site correspondent for China Tibet Information who assisted me in locating hard-to-find current information about Tibet.

Cover photo:
Pilgrim praying
among prayer
flags

Contents

Potala Palace

Monpa woman and child

Land of
Many Names

Tibet is landlocked and surrounded by mountains.

T HROUGH THE CENTURIES, TIBETAN AND NON-TIBETAN people have called the land of Tibet by many names. An ancient Buddhist legend from India tells of a peaceful land called Shambhala, or Shangri-La, that was hidden north of Mount Kailash in western Tibet. Wise men ruled in Shangri-La, and no one suffered from hunger, illness, or poverty. Perhaps best of all, no one got old or died in Shangri-La. Many explorers and peace-seeking pilgrims unsuccessfully searched for this heaven on earth. Instead, they found a land, a people, and a culture that are unique in the world.

Land of Snows and Roof of the World are other names for Tibet. They refer to Tibet's unusual geography. Snow-capped mountains—some of them the world's highest—almost completely encircle Tibet. The entire area of Tibet sits on the world's highest and largest plateau.

Opposite: **Tibet is the highest region in the world.**

Non-Tibetans called Tibet the Hidden Kingdom. High mountains hid the kingdom from outsiders. During much of its history, Tibet's rulers also made it difficult for outsiders to gain entry. At various times, however, Tibet's kings led their armies beyond the mountains, traders in caravans carried exotic goods into Tibet, and religious thinkers brought Buddhist ideas to the Hidden Kingdom.

After many years, Buddhism touched every aspect of Tibetan life, including how to treat the earth and plants and animals. People in neighboring countries and in other parts of the world began to call Tibet the World's Most Spiritual Land. Colorful prayer flags fluttered in the breeze at mountain passes

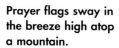

Prayer flags sway in the breeze high atop a mountain.

A novice monk does his schoolwork at the Drepung Monastery in Lhasa.

and from roofs of homes. At least one child from each family lived as a monk or a nun in one of the country's many monasteries. Lay people—those not of the clergy—as well as monks and nuns twirled prayer wheels. Buddhist monks called Dalai Lamas even ruled Tibet's government from 1642 to 1959.

The Chinese People's Liberation Army entering Lhasa in 1950

In 1950 the People's Liberation Army (PLA) of the People's Republic of China marched into Lhasa, Tibet's holy city and capital. Tibet became part of China and was renamed *Xizang*, which in Chinese means "Western Treasure House." Many Tibetans feel that China has been looting the Western Treasure House by slaughtering wildlife, overcutting forests, and digging for minerals. Since 1965, Tibet's official name has been the Tibet Autonomous Region (TAR). China set up autonomous regions, prefectures, and counties in areas where one ethnic group made up a majority of the population. In this case, the Tibetans are regarded as a minority ethnic group within the People's Republic of China. The Han Chinese form the ethnic majority.

The Beginning of the Question of Tibet

When China drew the boundaries of TAR, much of the land that Tibetans think of as part of Tibet was not included. Pre-1950, Tibet was made up of four provinces: Amdo, Kham, Ü-Tsang, and Ngari. Now, TAR includes Ü-Tsang, Ngari, and

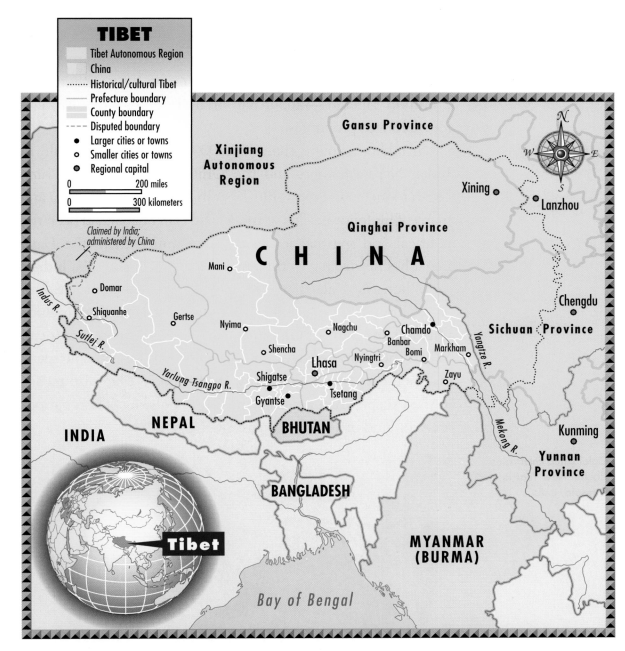

Geopolitical map of Tibet

part of western Kham. Amdo makes up all of China's Qinghai Province and part of China's Gansu Province. Eastern Kham is now part of China's Sichuan and Yunnan Provinces. Some 2 million Tibetans—about half of all Tibetans—live in these four Chinese provinces.

In addition, more than 130,000 Tibetans live in exile in India, Nepal, Europe, and the United States. When China began to increase its power in Tibet in 1959, the Dalai Lama and many of his followers fled to India. The Dalai Lama had been the political and spiritual leader of Tibet. Since then, the Dalai Lama has headed a government-in-exile in Dharamsala, India.

When the Dalai Lama and most other Tibetans speak of Tibet, they mean TAR and the areas of land that include Qinghai and parts of Gansu, Sichuan, and Yunnan Provinces. When the Chinese government and the Chinese people speak of Tibet, they mean TAR only. In this book Tibet also means TAR, except when dealing with Tibet's history. Then various areas of land are referred to as Tibet.

The Dalai Lama celebrates the Tibetan New Year in Dharamsala, India

More than fifty years have passed since the PLA entered Lhasa. It has been almost forty years since China formed TAR. During these years, most Tibetans have held the belief that Tibet was an independent country in 1950. According to them, Tibet is now an occupied country that has endured harsh rule under the People's Republic of China. They accuse the Chinese government of trying to wipe out Tibetan culture and of denying Tibetans their basic human rights. These Tibetans look forward to a time when Tibet will once again be independent.

On the other hand, China states that as early as the A.D. 600s Tibet was part of China. China admits that weak Chinese governments were not always able to control Tibet. For example, Tibetan armies sacked China's capital in 763. According to the Chinese government today, the actions of the PLA in 1950 simply rightfully reunited Tibet with China.

Since the 1980s, the Dalai Lama has no longer sought independence for Tibet. Instead, he suggests a middle course to solve the Tibet question. He proposes that all lands in China with large Tibetan populations be united under one governmental unit—a true Tibet Autonomous Region. He asks that the Tibetan people be allowed to rule themselves democratically. However, the enlarged TAR would remain part of China, with China taking care of TAR's relations with other countries and providing defense for Tibet. If this comes to pass, the Dalai Lama will end the government-in-exile, will return to Tibet, and will serve only as Tibet's religious leader.

A tourist group visits the Samye Monastery.

In the meantime, Tibet is no longer a Hidden Kingdom stuck in time, a mysterious, magical Shangri-La. Thousands of people from around the world visit Tibet each year. They realize that Tibet is a real place populated with real people who have real problems. Tourists and representatives from other countries also see the gap between rich and poor in Tibet and the destruction that has occurred under Chinese rule.

Tibetans remain proud of their cultural heritage—the Tibetan language, Tibetan Buddhism, and traditional ways of daily life—and make every effort to maintain it. At the same time, Tibetans are a part of the modern world. Now they must decide how to balance their traditions with modern ways as they seek a real voice in Tibet's government of the twenty-first century.

Monks walk past J.J. Disco, a sign of changing times in Tibet.

The Roof of the World

IBET'S LAND IS BEST KNOWN FOR ITS HIGH ALTITUDES, harsh climate, and rocky soil. Although those facts are true, Tibet also has fertile river valleys, grassy grazing lands, and alpine forests.

Located in south-central Asia, the Tibet Autonomous Region covers 471,662 square miles (1,221,600 square kilometers) of the southwestern part of the People's Republic of China. This region makes up about 13 percent of China's total area. In comparison to European countries, Tibet is a bit larger than France, Germany, and Italy combined. In North America, Montana and Texas combined are slightly smaller than Tibet, as is the Canadian Province of Ontario.

Most of Tibet borders other parts of China. To the north lies the Xinjiang Autonomous Region, also known as East Turkistan or Sinkiang Uighur. Qinghai Province is to the north and northeast; Sichuan Province, to the east; and Yunnan Province, to the southeast. The country of Myanmar (formerly Burma) also is to the southeast. To the south lie the countries of India, Nepal, and Bhutan. India also forms Tibet's western border.

Opposite: **Wildflowers flourish along Kangshung Glacier.**

Naming and Spelling Tibet's Geographical Features

Many of Tibet's geographical features, such as mountains, rivers, and lakes, are named for sacred beings or are simply a physical description of a feature. Tibet's physical features have not been named after people, as they are in most countries.

In addition, Tibet's geographical features can have two or three spellings depending on which original language—Tibetan, Chinese, Mongolian, or Sanskrit—is being translated into English. In this book the most commonly recognized English spelling is used.

How Tibet's Land Was Formed

About 100 million years ago, what is now Central Asia lay under the Tethys Sea. During that time a large piece of land that is now India was adrift in this sea. Then, about 40 million years ago, India slammed into and pushed under the softer land of Asia. Gradually, the bed of the Tethys Sea rose up and became the high Tibetan Plateau. By 13.5 million years ago, the Tibetan Plateau reached its present height of 16,400 feet (5,000 meters) above sea level. According to a recent study by a team of U.S., British, and Chinese geologists, the plateau will not become any higher.

The collision of India and Asia also forced the earth's crust to fold and be pushed upward thousands of feet. The Himalaya Mountains, which border southern Tibet, and a parallel range of mountains inside Tibet resulted from this folding and pushing. As the world's highest and youngest mountain range, the Himalaya continue to rise by 2 to 4 inches (5 to 10 centimeters) a year.

Tibet's Mountains

Tibet's rugged mountains almost completely encircle the Tibetan Plateau and have served a twofold purpose throughout Tibet's history. First, they kept the Tibetan people isolated from the rest of the world. This isolation made it possible for the unique Tibetan culture to develop. Second, the mountains kept invaders out of Tibet until the 1950s. For much of that time, Tibet was a buffer between its larger neighbors, India and China.

Mountains encircling Tibet provided protection and isolation during Tibet's development.

For Tibetans, mountains are sacred because they link the sky to the earth. Mount Kailash, at 22,027 feet (6,714 m), is Tibet's holiest mountain. Located in the Kailash range in far southwestern Tibet, Mount Kailash is hard to reach. However, both Tibetan Buddhists and Hindus from India try to make at least one pilgrimage to this mountain during their lifetime. Tibetans regard Mount Kailash as the central peak of the world and the protector of the Tibetan people. The Kailash and the Nyainqêntanglha ranges stand parallel to the Himalaya Mountains but are separated from the Himalaya by the Yarlung Tsangpo River valley.

One-third of the world's mountain peaks that are more than 23,000 feet (7,010 m) above sea level rise above Tibet. The mighty *Himalaya*, which means "Home of Snows" in Sanskrit, stretch 1,554 miles (2,500 km) along Tibet's southern boundary before curving north to form part of Tibet's western border. These mountains vary in width from 124 to 186 miles (200 to 300 km). Passes through the mountains are as high as

For Tibetans, Mount Kailash is a sacred spot where spiritual energy can be experienced.

Mount Everest, the highest peak in the world

18,560 feet (5,657 m) and are closed by snow in the winter. Sudden snowstorms at other times of the year also shut them down. Huge glaciers lie among the Himalayas' peaks.

On the border with Nepal, Mount Everest soars high above all the other Himalayan peaks. At 29,035 feet (8,850 m) above sea level, Everest is the highest point on earth. Tibetans call Everest *Chomolungma*, which means "Goddess Mother of the World." Including Mount Everest, five of the world's ten highest peaks stand on the Tibet-Nepal border. Fourth highest is Lhotse I, at 27,923 feet (8,511 m); fifth highest, Makalu I, at 27,824 feet (8,481 m); and ninth highest, Cho Oyu, at 26,750 feet (8,153 m).

Northwest of the Himalaya, the Karakorum Mountains, with an average elevation of 19,520 feet (5,950 m), form the rest of Tibet's western border with India. The Kunlun Mountains form Tibet's northern border. Mount Ulugh Muz Tag near Tibet's border with the Xinjiang Autonomous Region is the Kunluns' highest peak at 25,340 feet (7,724 m). With an average altitude of 20,000 feet (about 6,100 m) the Dangla Mountains provide part of Tibet's border with Qinghai Province to the northeast. In southeastern Tibet, the Hengduan Mountains run north to south.

Because TAR sits upon the Tibetan Plateau—the world's highest plateau—Tibet is sometimes called the Roof of the World. Altitudes on the plateau average about 16,000 feet (about 4,900 m) above sea level. Extending north and east from TAR into other parts of China, the Tibetan Plateau is also the world's largest plateau.

Within TAR's part of the Tibetan Plateau there are four geographic regions: the Chang Tang (Northern Plain), the far-western highlands, the Yarlung Tsangpo River valley in the south, and the southeastern river gorges. The two river regions are on lower elevations at the southern and eastern edges of the Tibetan Plateau. This part of the plateau is sometimes called the outer plateau.

Stretching west to east across the northern two-thirds of the Tibetan Plateau is the Chang Tang, with an average altitude of 15,000 feet (4,572 m). This region can be best described as a high-altitude desert, somewhat like the dry land in northern Nevada—only higher. Most of the Chang Tang has dry, rocky soil in which few plants can grow. Rivers flow for short distances through the Chang Tang. Its lakes are filled with saltwater left over from the Tethys Sea, an ancient sea. Tibetan Buddhists say that the tears of Tara, the goddess of compassion, formed these salty lakes. Mineral salts seep up through the Chang Tang's soil. Besides salt, the Chang Tang is a rich source of borax, gypsum, and quartz. In recent years, large deposits of oil, gas, and coal have been found on the Chang Tang.

A nomad with his pony on the Chang Tang

Few people have ever ventured into this area, let alone lived there. Along the Chang Tang's southern border, however, some of Tibet's nomad people find grazing land for their livestock. Hot springs near the town of Rongma also attract nomads, who bathe in the warm waters.

Although dry land is also found in the far-western highlands, this region's river valleys provide more grassland for nomads' livestock. In fact, the Indus and the Sutlej Rivers, which flow into India, have their sources in far-western Tibet's Kailash Mountain Range. Hot springs in the western highlands also provide clean water for nomads to bathe in. Geysers that shoot hot water several feet into the air are also found in this region.

The Yarlung Tsangpo River valley region forms along the Yarlung Tsangpo River as it flows east from the Kailash range through the southern part of the plateau. Tibet's most fertile land lies in this region, supporting large crops of barley and wheat. The Yarlung Tsangpo River valley is sometimes called the cradle of Tibetan civilization. Tibet's first line of kings took their name from the Yarlung. Today, this valley is home to the bulk of Tibet's population. Lhasa, Tibet's capital and largest city, is in the Yarlung Tsangpo River valley. Three of

Tibet's next-largest cities developed around monasteries in the Yarlung Tsangpo River valley: Shigatse, Tsetang, and Gyantse.

In Tibet's southeastern region, the Salween, the Mekong, and the Yangtze Rivers have cut deep gorges through the Hengduan Mountains. Because this region is at the lowest altitude of the Tibetan Plateau, thick forests and lush subtropical plants can grow there. Copper, gold, and bauxite are the region's major mineral deposits. Chamdo is the southeastern region's largest city.

Rivers and Lakes

Besides being the highest land in the world, the Tibetan Plateau is also the source of Asia's major rivers. The water for these rivers come from melted glaciers, ice, and snow, as well as rain and groundwater. As already mentioned, the Indus, the Sutlej, and the Yarlung Tsangpo begin in southwestern Tibet and wind their way into India. In Pakistan, west of India, the Sutlej joins the Indus, which empties into the Arabian Sea. In India the Yarlung Tsangpo is called the Brahmaputra. There it merges with the Ganges, which empties in the Bay of Bengal.

The fertile Yarlung Tsangpo River valley is known as Tibet's cradle of civilization.

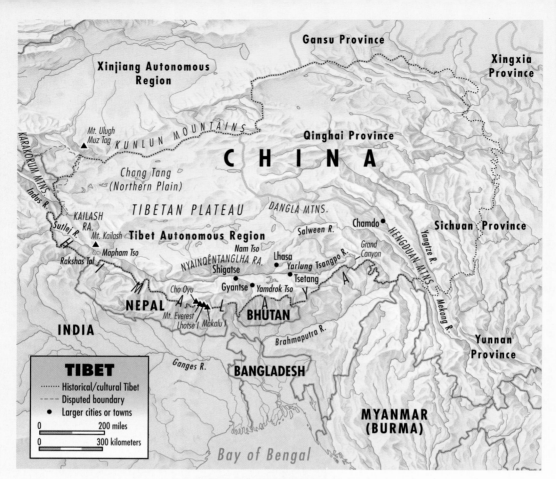

Tibet's Geographical Features

Area: 471,662 square miles (1,221,600 sq km)

World's Highest Elevation: Mount Everest (*Chomolungma*), 29,035 feet (8,850 m) above sea level, on the border with Nepal

Lowest Elevation: 5,297 feet (1,615 m) above sea level on the big bend of the Yarlung Tsangpo River

Average Elevation: 16,000 feet (about 4,900 m) above sea level

Longest River: Yarlung Tsangpo, flowing west to east 1,278 miles (2,057 km)

Largest Lake: Nam Tso, 811 square miles (2,100 sq km)

World's Highest Freshwater Lake: Mapham Tso, 15,000 feet (4,572 m) above sea level

Highest Annual Precipitation: 78 inches (198 cm) in the southeast

Lowest Annual Precipitation: Less than 2 inches (5 cm) in the north

Highest Average Temperature: 58°F (14°C)

Lowest Average Temperature: 24°F (−4°C)

Greatest Distance North to South: 620 miles (998 km)

Greatest Distance East to West: 2,030 miles (3,267 km)

Deepest Canyon: Yarlung Tsangpo Grand Canyon, 14,764 feet (4,500 m) deep

In Tibet, the Yarlung Tsangpo flows west to east for 1,278 miles (2,057 km). At an average altitude of 13,000 feet (3,962 m), this is the world's highest river. Where the Yarlung swings south, it has formed the Yarlung Tsangpo Grand Canyon. In a series of rapids, the river falls about 11,000 feet (3,350 m). The crashing water has etched the world's deepest canyon, 14,764 feet (4,500 m) deep.

On the southeastern plateau, the Salween River begins on its way to Myanmar and into the Gulf of Martaban. The southeastern Tibetan Plateau's other major rivers, the Mekong and the Yangtze, begin in Qinghai Province before entering Tibet. The Yangtze then turns east and winds across the entire width of China until it empties into the East China Sea near Shanghai. The Mekong flows southeast through Tibet, southern China, and Southeast Asia until it reaches Vietnam, where it empties into the South China Sea.

The Yarlung Tsangpo River flows through the Yarlung Tsangpo Grand Canyon, the world's deepest canyon.

The Yangtze River as it flows through the Tibetan Plateau

A dramatic view of Yamdrok Tso, Tibet's largest freshwater lake

With more than 1,500 lakes, Tibet has one-third of all the lakes in China. They are known for a deep turquoise-blue color caused by mineral deposits and the bright Tibetan sunlight. Most of them are on the Chang Tang. Nam Tso, northwest of Lhasa, is Tibet's largest lake and the second-largest saltwater lake in China. South of Lhasa lies Yamdrok Tso, Tibet's largest freshwater lake.

In southwestern Tibet lie the twin lakes of Mapham Tso, also known as Lake Manasarovar, and Rakshas Tal. Mapham Tso is the world's highest freshwater lake and, more importantly, one of Tibetan Buddhism's holiest sites. Mapham Tso is shaped like the sun, and its waters are some of the purest on earth. It is not far from holy Mount Kailash, whose reflection is caught in the lake. In contrast, Rakshas Tal has a crescent-moon shape and dark, wild waters. These two lakes represent the balance that Buddhists believe is necessary in life.

Climate

Tibet is one of the few places on earth where a person can get sunburned and frostbitten at the same time. High altitudes and clear skies with bright sunlight can quickly lead to a sunburn. This can also happen when the sun reflects off snow. If the temperature drops below freezing on a sunny day, unprepared people in Tibet might experience frostbite on their fingers, toes, or faces.

In general, Tibet's climate is cool and dry. The high altitudes of the Tibetan Plateau and the surrounding mountains, however, give Tibet a climate of extremes. The high Himalaya Mountains, for example, prevent the rains from the monsoon winds that hit southern Asia from reaching the Tibetan Plateau. High altitudes also make Tibet's air thinner than in other places in the world. That happens because at high altitudes the air has less oxygen. At average altitudes, Tibetan air has about 50 percent less oxygen than air in most of the rest of the world.

The Chang Tang experiences the harshest climate conditions. Less than 2 inches (5 cm) of rain fall there each year. Much of the snow that falls on the Chang Tang evaporates because of the dry air. Throughout the year on the Chang Tang, strong winds cause severe dust storms. July temperatures on the Chang Tang may be 86° Fahrenheit (30° Celsius) during the day and drop to 5°F (–15°C) at night. January temperatures can go as low as minus 30°F (–34°C).

The Yarlung Tsangpo River valley has the mildest weather, with July temperatures of 70°F (21°C) and January temperatures of 47°F (8°C). About 20 inches (51 cm) of rain and snow fall in the valley each year. The southeastern river gorge region is at a lower altitude of about 3,900 feet (1,189 m). This region has a subtropical climate with high summer temperatures and heavy rains of about 78 inches (198 cm).

The Land of Snows receives an average of 18 inches (46 cm) of rain and snow a year. However, snow at altitudes of between 16,000 and 20,000 feet (4,877 and 6,096 m) never melts. Land at these elevations is called the permanent snow line.

Looking at Tibetan Cities

Shigatse (above), whose name translates as "Best in the Land," is Tibet's second-largest city. It lies on the Yarlung Tsangpo River west of Lhasa at an altitude of 12,795 feet (3,900 m). Shigatse has an average July temperature of 61°F (16°C) and an average January temperature of 23°F (–5°C). The city grew around the Tashilhunpo Monastery, which was founded in 1447 by Gendun Drup. Later he was recognized as the First Dalai Lama. From the 1600s until the present the monastery has been the seat of the Panchen Lama. Today, the city has a large Han Chinese population, and several Chinese army bases surround it. The Tibetan part of town has a large marketplace that sells Tibetan boots, hats, stirrups, and woven cloth, as well

as dried legs of lamb. The Gangyen Carpet Factory allows visitors to watch weavers hand-looming carpets with detailed designs.

Tsetang, whose name means "Playground," is Tibet's third-largest city. At an elevation of 11,800 feet (about 3,600 m), it is southeast of Lhasa on the Yarlung Tsangpo River at the base of Mount Gongbori. According to Tibet's creation myth, in a cave of this mountain a saintly monkey mated with an ogress to give birth to the Tibetan people. The first kings of Tibet—the Yarlung Dynasty—ruled from the Tsetang area. Some of these kings are buried in the nearby Valley of the Kings. Tibet's first palace, Yumbu Lagang, was built south of Tsetang. Although it was destroyed during the Chinese Cultural Revolution, it has been rebuilt. Tibet's first Buddhist temple, Trandruk, and its first Buddhist monastery, Samye, are also near Tsetang. The town itself was founded in 1351. Today Tsetang is the capital of the TAR's Lhoka Prefecture and has a large Han Chinese population. The old Tibetan quarters are surrounded by Chinese concrete-block buildings and karaoke bars.

Chamdo, whose name means "Where Rivers Join," is Tibet's fourth-largest city. It is located in far eastern Tibet where the branches of the Mekong River come together. This city is the center of the Khampa people's homeland. These Tibetans are known as fierce warriors who fought bravely against the Chinese during the 1950 invasion. Today Khampa and Chinese traders sell goods in the Tromzikhang market, where shoppers get good buys on Tibetan textiles and books. The best-known

building in town is the Galden Jampaling Monastery. Founded in the early 1400s, the monastery was destroyed twice by the Chinese and rebuilt both times.

Gyantse (below), Tibet's fifth-largest city, is located on the Nyang River southwest of Lhasa at an altitude of 12,959 feet (3,950 m). Founded in the 1300s by King Pelden Sangpo, Gyantse became the center of Tibet's wool trade and the gateway to India. Gyantse escaped much of the destruction that other Tibetan cities suffered in the 1960s, it still feels like a small Tibetan town. The main attractions are a huge fort, the Pelkor Choede Monastery, and the Kumbum, Tibet's largest chorten, or stupa. The Gyantse Carpet Factory is the main business in town. Weavers continue the town's long tradition of making hand-woven carpets. Each summer, the town comes alive during the five-day Horse Festival in July or August.

The Delicate Environment

32

A mountain forest ablaze with color

ALTHOUGH TIBET'S high altitudes and harsh climate tend to make life difficult, many kinds of plants and animals manage to live and even thrive on the Tibetan Plateau. Scientists have found about 200 species of mammals, more than 500 species of birds, and several species of reptiles, amphibians, and insects. In addition, more than 12,000 species of green plants and 5,000 of fungi grow in Tibet. About 80 percent of these species of plants and animals live in the lower altitudes and warmer climate of southeastern Tibet. Only about 10 percent of these species live on the Chang Tang.

The Southeastern Mountains

Nyingtri Prefecture in southeastern Tibet is covered by a huge forest. In fact, 65 percent of Tibet's forestland is in this mountainous region. One part of this prefecture is called the Lunang Forest. Larches and evergreens such as firs, pines, and spruces are some of the more common trees found there. Rarer trees such as camphor and white sandalwood also grow in Lunang. A variety of colorful flowers blooms among the trees. Chrysanthemums, peonies, wild peach blossoms, and twenty-five varieties of azaleas blossom there in the spring. In the summer, large amounts of edible mushrooms sprout up.

Opposite: **A yak finds good grazing on the plateau.**

The red panda makes its home in southeastern Tibet.

The Metok Nature Preserve along the Yarlung Tsangpo River is also in southeastern Tibet. This mountainous preserve has 340 frost-free days and receives about 78 inches (198 cm) of rain each year. Because such lush conditions allow more than 3,000 species of plants to thrive, the preserve is sometimes called a Museum of Plants. At least a dozen kinds of bamboo and more than eighty types of orchids grow in lower altitudes of the preserve. Primrose and blue felwert bloom in the high mountain meadows. Chinese hemlock, spruce, oriental white oak, and chinquapin are the major trees at middle altitudes. Much of the forest's ground is covered with moss that climbs up the trees' trunks.

An interesting animal in the southeast's bamboo forest is the red panda. This long-tailed mammal with pointed ears and masked face is the size of a large cat. Because it eats bamboo, it was once thought to be a relative of the giant panda. Now, however, the red panda is grouped as a raccoon.

Bharals, or blue sheep,
on a rocky hillside

Life in the Himalaya

The many altitudes of the Himalaya provide homes for several kinds of plants and animals. The bharal, or blue sheep, is actually half goat. Its short legs help it climb the steep Himalayan slopes. Thick coats keep the bharals warm in winter. Unfortunately, snow leopards and wolves prowl these mountains and feed on the bharals. Lammergeiers, or bearded vultures, eat the bones of animals such as the bharal. They break the bones into pieces small enough to eat by dropping them from great heights, so that they smash on the rocky mountain ledges.

A lammergeier, or
bearded vulture

In the spring, flowers bloom in the Himalaya. More than 500 species of rhododendrons and azaleas burst forth in a variety of colors. The rhododendrons and azaleas that grace many American and European gardens originally came from Tibet. At the highest altitudes where plants can grow, the rhododendron bushes are shorter, and twisted from the wind. The

Rhododendrons bloom during an early mountain spring.

Himalaya blue poppy

Himalaya blue poppy is a rare flower with bluish-purple petals that feel like paper.

Plants and Animals of the Chang Tang

Although the Chang Tang is mainly stony or salty windswept land, about fifty kinds of plants grow there. Sage, tansy, ephedra, and other low-growing shrubs are found in river drainage areas. Juniper bushes cluster together along the shores of Nam Tso, the large saltwater lake. Drought-resistant

Mythical Animals of Tibet

The *seng-ge*, or snow lion, with its turquoise mane and tail, is the symbol of Tibet. This mythical beast is said to live in Tibet's Himalaya, jumping from one peak to another and magically never touching the snow.

Another beast haunts the Himalaya but leaves its footprints behind. This is the yeti, a huge, hairy man/beast, also known as the abominable snow-man. In the northwestern United States, a relative of the yeti is called Sasquatch, or bigfoot. Although there is no proof that such a beast really exists, some explorers, hunters, and trekkers claim to have seen its footprints.

One of the smallest inhabitants of the Chang Tang is the pika.

A black-necked crane

grasses such as feather grass, poa, quack grass, and sheep's fescue grow on the southern edges of the Chang Tang.

Small herds of chirus (Tibetan antelopes), Tibetan argali (wild sheep), bharals, gazelles, kiangs (Tibetan wild asses), and Tibetan wild yaks graze on the grasses of the Chang Tang. A few snow leopards and wolves also live on the Chang Tang. Other predatory animals include the Tibetan brown bear and lynx. One of the smallest animals on the Chang Tang is the pika. This brown, furry plant-eater looks like a guinea pig. It makes a squeaky sound to warn other pikas about danger. The lakes and marshes of the Chang Tang provide breeding grounds for the black-necked crane. This bird was near extinction in the 1980s, but by the year 2000, about 5,500 of them again lived in Tibet.

Why the Chiru Is Endangered

The chiru, or Tibetan antelope, has been declared an endangered species. In the early 1900s, about a million chiru lived on the Chang Tang. By the late 1990s, there were only between 65,000 and 72,000. Most of the chirus have been shot by poachers, who kill them for their valuable wool. The chiru's wool is made into shahtoosh shawls that are smuggled into European and North American countries. These soft, cashmerelike shawls are illegally sold for thousands of dollars. In the United States, the federal government has fined retail-store owners up to $175,000 for selling these shawls. As more shoppers become aware of the connection between endangered chirus and shahtoosh shawls, perhaps poachers in Tibet will lose their market for chiru wool.

Tibetan Buddhist View of the Environment

Throughout most of their history Tibetans have lived in harmony with their environment. They had a personal relationship between themselves and the earth. In 1642 the Fifth Dalai Lama issued what is believed to be the first law in history that protects the environment. Following Buddhist teachings, he called on Tibetans to respect all life, including plants and animals. Buddhists believe in a cycle of life, death, and rebirth in which all living things have many lives. For example, an insect could be reborn as a person, or a person could be reborn as a dog. For this reason, most Tibetans do not hunt or fish or slaughter domesticated animals on a large scale. They believe that it is better to kill one yak because its meat will feed many, than to kill several chickens or catch many fish to feed the same number of people.

Tibetans also protected plant life and mineral resources. They only cut down trees when no other building materials were available and then planted seeds for new trees. Plants that they picked for medicines quickly regrew. Other than plowing fields to grow crops, Tibetans did not dig into the earth so as not to disturb spirits who lived there. They gathered salt that was on top of the earth. They picked gold, silver, and turquoise from streams.

Environmental Challenges

Many of the actions that China took in Tibet after its 1950 invasion went totally against the Tibetan Buddhist way of interacting with the environment. Chinese soldiers shot thousands of yaks and antelopes. Some were used for food to supply the Chinese army, but many animals were shot for sport only. Tibetans also tell of soldiers dynamiting rivers to bring fish to the surface and blasting birds out of trees. The greatest damage done to the environment has been the clear-cutting of Tibet's forests. Some reports show that more than two-thirds of the forests have been cut down. Many of the trees grew on slopes and held the soil in place. With the trees gone, rains now cause landslides and floods. Much of the soil finds its way into Tibet's rivers that flow into other Asian countries. Chinese policies have

Trees have been planted in the Lhasa Valley to control land erosion.

also exploited Tibet's natural resources of coal and gold. Strip-mining of these minerals destroyed grasses that once covered the ground. Yaks and other livestock now have less grazing land.

By the late 1990s, China realized the damage that had been done and how it was affecting Tibetans, as well as parts of China downstream from Tibet's rivers. Regulations were passed to better protect Tibet's environment. Unfortunately, by that time more than 100 species of animals had become endangered. They include the Tibetan wild yak, the Tibetan argali sheep, the chiru (Tibetan antelope), the snow leopard, and the kiang (Tibetan wild ass). Overhunting by the Chinese army, poachers, and expeditions of tourists are the main cause of the decline of these species. Recent harsh winters with deep snows on the Chang Tang also wiped out large numbers of kiangs and chirus. Other animals died off because their forests or grasslands had been destroyed. It will take many years to undo the damage to Tibet's environment.

Many people outside of Tibet are also worried about its environment. People throughout Asia depend on a clean environment in Tibet because their water supply comes from rivers that begin on the Tibetan Plateau. The plateau's location and altitude also affect weather patterns in the rest of the world.

Nature Reserves

At one time, all of Tibet would have been considered a national park or a nature reserve. The Tibetan people protected the land, plants, and animals because of their Buddhist beliefs.

The Chang Tang Nature Reserve, the world's second-largest reserve, is home to protected wildlife.

Since 1950, however, much of Tibet's environment has been harmed. China's central government along with the local government have attempted to reverse this harm by setting aside land in nature reserves. More than 25 percent of Tibet is now part of about fourteen nature reserves. Unlike many reserves and national parks in other parts of the world, those in Tibet have people living in them.

The Chang Tang Nature Reserve, at 128,500 square miles (332,815 sq km), is the world's second-largest reserve. Only Greenland National Park is bigger. Chirus, gazelles, and wild yaks are some animals protected in the Chang Tang Nature Reserve. Nomads graze their yaks, horses, sheep, and goats on the reserve's grasses. The Chomolungma Nature Reserve includes Mount Everest and four other of the world's highest peaks. About 67,000 Tibetans farm and herd livestock in this reserve. Wildlife that are protected in this reserve include the snow leopard and the civet.

An Endangered Medicinal Plant

What is both a plant and an animal and found between 13,000 and 14,500 feet (3,962 and 4,420 m) above sea level? Its scientific name is *Cordyceps sinensis*, but Tibetans call this strange being *yarsa-kumbu* (right). It occurs when spores from a certain kind of fungus land on a caterpillar that has burrowed into the ground. The fungus enters the caterpillar's body and then pushes out of the caterpillar's head. In the fall Tibetans crawl on their hands and knees looking for this plant-animal. After gathering the black fungus, Tibetans dry and grind it, then mix the fungus with milk

or honey. This mixture, which increases the strength of men and yaks, is worth up to $412 per pound. Because yarsa-kumbu is so valuable, it has been over-gathered and now is hard to find.

Tibet's Dogs

Tibet has been the homeland of several breeds of dogs. The small Lhasa apso, Tibetan terrier, and Tibetan spaniel (below left) were mainly pets. Their shrill barks, however, made them watchdogs in the homes of wealthy Tibetans. The Lhasa apso and the Tibetan terrier were thought to bring good luck and were often given as gifts. The Tibetan mastiff (right), weighing more than 100 pounds (45 kilograms), warned off human intruders and scared wild animals away from livestock at night with a deep, foghorn bark.

Since the early 1900s, many of these animals have been taken out of Tibet. Their descendants are now pets and show dogs in Europe and the United States. When the Chinese Communists took over Tibet, soldiers shot many of the dogs. To

the Communists, dogs were a symbol of corrupt, decadent living. In Tibet today, the mastiff is still used as a guard dog in monasteries, villages, and nomad camps. The smaller dogs are again living as family pets in villages and cities.

Kings, Lamas, and Communists

LITTLE IS KNOWN ABOUT THE EARLY HISTORY OF TIBET and its people. The first written history of Tibet dates only from the A.D. 600s. Information from archaeology has been limited because Buddhist beliefs prevented digging into the earth. In recent years, however, archaeologists have found evidence that people lived in Tibet at least 30,000 years ago.

Opposite: **Ruins of the Guge Kingdom, a kingdom founded in the tenth century that lasted for 700 years.**

Stone knives and hide scrapers show that 20,000 to 30,000 years ago people on the Chang Tang were hunters. At that time, the Chang Tang had a warmer, wetter climate. Near Lhasa, a rocky mountain slope that was mud 20,000 years ago has revealed the handprints and footprints of adults and children. North of Chamdo stand the remains of a 5,000-year-old, two-story building. It is believed that farming people built that structure. They kept farm animals on the first floor and lived on the second floor. Other remains show that these people made pottery and used needles made from bone.

Throughout these early years, clans and tribes of people moved from Central Asia across the Tibetan Plateau. Gradually, individual tribes gained control of their own areas of Tibet and set up kingdoms. For centuries, the chiefs of these kingdoms waged war with one another until the Yarlung chiefs united Tibet for the first time.

The Yarlung Dynasty: Myths and Stories

Tibetan histories name Nyatri Tsenpo as Tibet's first king during the 400s B.C. Legends tell that Nyatri Tsenpo came down from heaven on a sky cord and landed in the Yarlung Tsangpo River valley near present-day Tsetang. Tibet's first kings are said to have entered and left this world via a sky cord, which made them divine. About 100 B.C., a servant tricked the eighth king, Drigum Tsenpo, into cutting his sky cord. After losing his link to divinity, Drigum Tsenpo was then killed by his servant. From that point on according to the legend, the Yarlung Dynasty's kings were mortal men. They were buried in tombs in the Yarlung Tsangpo River valley.

According to the legends, the kings of the Yarlung Dynasty ruled from their fortress called Yumbu Lagang, near present-day Tsetang. Between 50 B.C. and A.D. 300, they introduced

Yumbu Lagang Palace was the first palace of the Yarlung kings.

farming with irrigated fields, and domesticated animals. Trade took place with neighboring dynasties in what later became the Tibetan provinces of Amdo and Kham. An upper class of landholding nobles grew. Under them were serfs who worked the land. The Yarlung kings developed a tax system based on lands held and farm goods produced. At this time, people in the Yarlung Tsangpo River valley practiced the Bon religion.

The Yarlung Dynasty: Factual History Begins

About A.D. 570, Namri Songtsen, the thirty-second Yarlung king, came to power. Ruling through a power base of the nobles, Namri Songtsen began to unite Tibet. He brought central Tibet under his control and moved his army into the borderlands of northwestern China. Chinese histories from that time say that Namri Songtsen's army had 100,000 soldiers. During his reign, the Yarlung Dynasty made diplomatic contacts with rulers in China and Mongolia. About 630 Namri Songtsen was assassinated by nobles.

Songtsen Gampo followed his father as the next Yarlung king and ruled until 650. He fully united Tibet by bringing the western kingdom of Zhangzhung under Yarlung control. He then extended Tibet's borders into China, India, and Nepal. To prevent further warfare with China and Nepal, Songtsen Gampo demanded and received princess brides from both countries. Under the king's direction, Thonmi Sambhota went to India and developed an alphabet and written script to express the spoken Tibetan language. The new script was used to write down Songtsen Gampo's law code and the first history

Above left: **An early depiction of the Potala Palace**

Above right: **This pillar commemorates the 821 treaty between Tibet and China.**

of Tibet. Songtsen Gampo also moved the capital to Lhasa and began building the Potala Palace on Red Hill.

After Songtsen Gampo's death, Tibet's conflicts with China resumed. By 680, the Yarlung king's armies had pushed into what is now Yunnan Province, and in 763 they occupied Xian, the ancient Chinese capital. Finally in 821, a treaty defined the Tibetan-Chinese border. Stone pillars with the treaty on them were erected at the border. One was also placed in front of the Jokhang Temple in Lhasa, where it still stands. Part of the treaty says:

> *Tibet and China shall abide by the frontiers of which they are now in occupation. All to the east is the country of Great China; and all to the west is, without question, the country of Great Tibet. . . . Tibetans shall be happy in Tibet, and Chinese shall be happy in China.*

By this time Buddhism had become the official religion of Tibet. A conflict then arose between followers of Bon and followers of Buddhism. In 836, Langdarma, an anti-Buddhist, killed his brother, King Ralpachen. The new king destroyed Buddhist writings, temples, and monasteries. Buddhist monks fled to the east and west. In 842, a Buddhist monk killed King Langdarma. With his death, the Yarlung Dynasty ended, and Tibet again was divided into separate kingdoms.

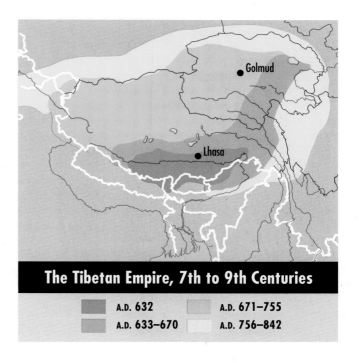

The Tibetan Empire, 7th to 9th Centuries

	A.D. 632		A.D. 671–755
	A.D. 633–670		A.D. 756–842

Revival of Buddhism

After the collapse of the Yarlung Dynasty, some Buddhist men fled east to Kham and were ordained as monks. By the late 900s they began returning to central Tibet, where they built new monasteries with the support of Buddhist nobles. Other Buddhist monks found favor and protection in the western kingdom of Guge. The kings built temples and monasteries. In 1042 King Yeshe O invited Atisha, a famous Buddhist in India, to come and teach about Buddhism. Later Atisha traveled to Netang, near Lhasa. There his followers built a monastery and founded the Kadampa order of Tibetan Buddhism.

Other orders of Tibetan Buddhism were founded between the late 1000s and the 1400s. The Sakyapa and the Kagyupa

The Three Religious Kings

Songtsen Gampo (who ruled from 630 to 650), Trisong Detsen (755–797), and Ralpachen (817–836) are known as the Three Religious Kings because they officially supported Buddhism. Buddhism first came to Tibet with Songtsen Gampo's Nepalese and Chinese wives—both Buddhists. Each wife brought a statue of the Buddha as a gift for the king. Songtsen Gampo built the Jokhang and Ramoche temples in Lhasa to house these statues. He also had Thonmi Sambhota begin translating the teachings of the Buddha from the Indian language of Sanskrit into the new Tibetan written language.

Trisong Detsen established Buddhism as the state religion. He invited Buddhist scholars, such as Padmasambhava from India, to teach in Tibet. He also backed the building of Samye, Tibet's first Buddhist monastery. During his reign, a debate at Samye about Chinese versus Indian Buddhism ended with India's version of Buddhism being adopted for Tibet. During another contest, Buddhism was shown as more powerful than Bon.

Under Ralpachen, Buddhist monks gained power as ministers, or advisers, in the king's government. Ralpachen donated large amounts of land to Buddhist monasteries. Those lands were no longer taxed. The tax burden was passed on to other landowners. He gave each monk huge households with many servants. Such favoritism toward the Buddhist monks set the nobles and Bon priests against Ralpachen.

were the first orders. A suborder called the Karma Kagyupa developed under the Kagyupa order. The Karmapa, or Karma Kagyupa, invented the idea of reincarnated lamas. Reincarnation is the belief that after death a person is reborn in a new body. The Karma Kagyupa used this idea to choose their leaders, or abbots. This means that when the first abbot died, he was reborn in the body of a baby. When this child was found, he was trained to be the next abbot and was called *lama*, which means "great teacher." Followers of the early scholar Padmasambhava were called the *Nyingmapa*, or Ancient Ones. The last main order to develop was the Gelukpa. It was based on the Kadampa order, which then became less important. Each order emphasized different parts of Buddhist teaching and had its own monasteries.

The growth of Buddhism in Tibet gave rise to new Buddhist teachings and orders. One great Tibetan Buddhist master was Tsong Kha Pa, founder of the Gelukpa order.

The Tibetan Buddhist orders were supported by different families of nobles. As the orders attracted more students who became monks and built more monasteries, their power increased. In time, the leaders of the orders became more powerful than the nobles. Some leaders were ordinary monks who became abbots and ran the monasteries. Other Buddhist leaders were abbots by birth. They were called lamas.

In the early 1200s, Mongolian forces moved through Central Asia and eventually invaded Tibet. The Mongols saw that the abbots and lamas were powerful and respected in Tibet. Beginning in 1247, Mongolian leaders formed a patron-priest relationship with leaders of the Sakyapa order. As the Mongol leader's representative, the Sakyapa lama or abbot kept Tibet loyal to the Mongols. The Mongols in turn protected Tibet from other invaders. Eventually, Kublai Khan made Buddhism the official religion of the Mongol Empire, which included China from 1279 to 1368. In China, the Mongols were called the Yuan Dynasty.

The Sakyapas remained in power until 1350 when Changchub Gyaltsen, a Kagyupa monk, forcefully defeated them. Eighteen years later the Chinese overthrew the Mongolian Yuan Dynasty, and the Mongols' patron-priest alliance in Tibet ended. Leaders of the Kagyupa order held spiritual and political power over Tibet until 1435. At that time princes of Rinpung, southwest of Lhasa, came to power. This dynasty controlled Tibet until 1565, following which the Tsang Dynasty of kings ruled Tibet from Shigatse. The Karma suborder of the Kagyupa provided spiritual leadership for Tibet under the Tsang.

By the 1570s, the Gelukpa order, with Tibet's largest monastery—the Drepung Monastery in Lhasa—had attracted the attention of the Mongols. The third Drepung abbot was the lama Sonam Gyatso. In 1578, the Mongol leader added *dalai*, which means "ocean of wisdom," to Sonam Gyatso's title of lama. Although he was the first person with the title Dalai Lama, Sonam Gyatso became the Third Dalai Lama. The title was extended back to honor his two previous incarnations—Gendun Drup and Gendun Gyatso.

When the Third Dalai Lama died in 1588 he reincarnated in the body of the great-grandson of the Mongol leader. The Tsang kings and their Karmapa supporters felt threatened by the Mongol-Gelukpa alliance. In 1611, the Tsang king attacked the Drepung and Sera monasteries in Lhasa. The Fourth Dalai Lama fled and died in exile five years later. Some Gelukpas tried to keep the peace between the Tsang and the Mongols. However, in 1642 the Mongols with the support of the Fifth Dalai Lama defeated the Tsang king.

Sonam Gyatso, the First Dalai Lama

The Great Fifth Dalai Lama was both spiritual teacher and political leader of Tibet.

The Great Fifth

Ngawang Lobsang Gyatso, the Fifth Dalai Lama, is usually called the Great Fifth. He was both the spiritual and the political leader of Tibet. As political leader, he made Lhasa the capital. With the Mongols' help he brought all of Tibet under his control—from the Kailash area in the west to Kham in the east. He set up a government that included monks and

Tibet's Dynasties

Yarlung Kings Dynasty	5th century B.C.–A.D. 842
Period of Disunity	842–1244
Sakyapa Order Dynasty	1244–1350
Kagyupa Order Dynasty	1350–1435
Rinpung Princes Dynasty	1435–1565
Tsang Kings Dynasty	1565–1642
Rule of the Dalai Lamas	1642–1959

nobles. This system of government lasted until 1959. As Tibet's spiritual leader, he built new monasteries and expanded the great Gelukpa monasteries of Ganden, Drepung, and Sera. The Great Fifth also expanded the Potala Palace.

When the Great Fifth died in 1682, his regent kept it a secret for thirteen years so the Potala Palace could be completed. The regent also did not want the Manchus to know that an adult Dalai Lama was no longer on the throne. Regents usually ruled Tibet while a child Dalai Lama was being trained and educated.

The Manchus and the British

In 1644, the Manchus had taken over China and formed the Qing Dynasty. They were looking for any excuse to take over Tibet. Also at this time, the Mongols hoped to gain power again in Tibet. The Manchus encouraged the Mongols to invade Tibet. When they did, in 1705, the Mongols killed the regent and kidnapped the Sixth Dalai Lama, who died shortly thereafter. In 1717, Buddhist Mongols invaded Tibet to avenge the Dalai Lama's death. The Manchus used the Mongol's invasion as an excuse to invade Tibet and restore order. In 1720, the Manchu emperor sent troops to Lhasa, drove out the Mongols, and declared Tibet a protectorate of China. In 1788, China closed Tibet to all foreigners. Chinese officials controlled Tibet until 1911. In that year, Chinese revolutionaries overthrew the Manchu/Qing Dynasty and set up a republic in China.

Actually, for most of the 1800s into the early 1900s, China's government was so busy with its own problems that it left Tibet alone. During this time, most of the Dalai Lamas died before they were old enough to rule. Regents governed in their place until the Thirteenth Dalai Lama received full power in 1895.

The Dalai Lama escaping from the Chinese and entering British India

In the late 1800s, Great Britain began knocking on Tibet's southern door. India, Tibet's neighbor to the south, was part of the British Empire, and Britain wanted to open Tibet for trade. The Dalai Lama's government refused. In 1903, British colonel Francis Younghusband led troops into Tibet and captured Lhasa. The Dalai Lama fled to Mongolia but returned in 1907 and opened Tibet to trade with the British. Before the Manchus lost power in China, they invaded Tibet to push the British out. This time the Dalai Lama fled to British protection in India. The Manchus lost power in China in 1911 and by the end of 1912 had been thrown out of Tibet. The Dalai Lama returned to Lhasa in 1913.

When the Dalai Lama returned to Tibet in 1913 he declared Tibet an independent nation. As an independent country, Tibet issued money, stamps, and passports, had its own flag, and made agreements with other countries. In 1914, the Simla Conference took place to resolve Tibet's border issues with British-controlled India and China. Britain agreed on the Tibet-India border and thereby recognized Tibet as an independent country. However, Britain also acknowledged that China had a special relationship with Tibet. China refused to take part in

Delegates to the 1914 Simla Conference worked to resolve Tibet's border issues.

the conference, so its border with Tibet remained unclear. By this time, parts of Amdo and Kham were already under China's control. Over the next several years, China took even more land in these provinces.

With the help of British advisers, the Dalai Lama began a program to reform and modernize the country. Tibet's government, economy, and society had stayed the same for hundreds of years. Most of the people were serfs. Monasteries, nobles, and government officials owned the land that the serfs worked. Serfs had to give their crops to the landowner and pay taxes to the landowner. Even though landowners set aside land for serfs to work for themselves, the serfs did not own that

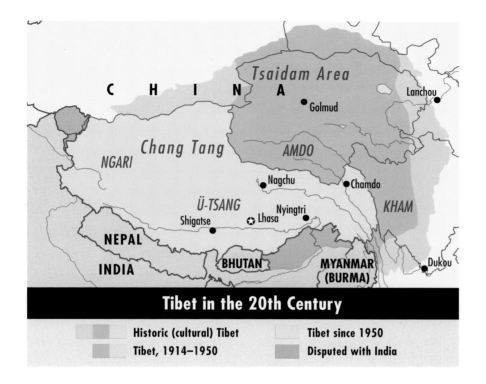

Tibet in the 20th Century

Historic (cultural) Tibet   Tibet since 1950

Tibet, 1914–1950   Disputed with India

land. To correct this system, the Dalai Lama changed the laws so serfs could own land and would not have to pay so many taxes. The monks and nobles were afraid of losing their power and objected to these reforms.

To enable Tibet to defend itself, the Dalai Lama also established an army. Because the monasteries had monk-soldiers, they saw the nonmonk army as a threat to their power. The Dalai Lama further tried to modernize Tibet by building telegraph lines and a hydroelectric power plant. Tibet's officials also objected to these actions. The government's main concern was supporting the abbots, lamas, and monks in the monasteries.

In 1933, the Thirteenth Dalai Lama died with Tibet still in need of reform and modernization. The reincarnated Dalai

Four-year-old Tenzin Gyatso, the Fourteenth Dalai Lama

Lama was found as a two-year-old child in Chinese-controlled Amdo. When he took the throne as the Fourteenth Dalai Lama in 1940, he was only four years old. He should have been eighteen before taking on his duties of political leadership. However, the invasion of Tibet by Chinese Communist forces from 1950 to 1951 caused the Dalai Lama to begin his reign at only age sixteen.

China Gains Control

In 1949, Mao Zedong and the Chinese Communists overthrew the Chinese Republic. They were determined to bring Tibet under Chinese control once again. According to the Communists, all people were workers and religion was poison.

In May 1951, Tibet's representatives in Beijing, China, were forced to sign the Seventeen-Point Agreement on Measures for the Peaceful Liberation of Tibet. That agreement basically said two things. First, Tibet would lose its independence, but the Dalai Lama's government would remain in power and Tibet could keep its language and religion. Second, China would take care of foreign and military affairs and would create a new economy by building factories, hospitals, roads, and schools. By September 1951, Mao's People's Liberation Army (PLA) controlled Kham and had marched into Lhasa.

Road building started first, so truckloads of Chinese soldiers could "liberate" Tibet. Because such large numbers of soldiers had to be fed, Tibet's food supply was soon gone. In Kham, the Communists had started forcing Tibetans to swear loyalty to Communist China. The Chinese had also begun dismantling the Dalai Lama's government. Because of these actions, thousands of people from all parts of Tibet rose up in revolt in Lhasa on March 10, 1959. They were in the capital for the Tibetan New Year Festival. The Dalai Lama tried to mediate between his people and the Chinese, but the Chinese bombed his summer palace, the Norbulingka. On March 17, the Dalai Lama left Lhasa and fled to India. He has not been back since. Thousands of Tibetans followed him into exile.

During the Lhasa uprising, about 10,000 to 15,000 Tibetans were killed. Many ancient buildings were destroyed or damaged, including the Norbulingka Palace, the Potala Palace, the Jokhang Temple, and the Sera Monastery. After the revolt, the Chinese Communists cracked down hard on Tibet, just as they were already doing in China. The Dalai

Tibetan monks surrender to Chinese troops in Lhasa, 1959.

Lama's government was abolished. All land owned by monasteries and nobles was seized. Monks and nobles had to attend "struggle sessions." During these sessions, people were tortured and beaten until they came around to the Communist way of thinking. Many monks and nuns were thrown in prison. Farmers were forced to

grow wheat and rice instead of their traditional barley. Wheat and rice did not grow well in Tibet, and soon there wasn't enough food. By 1962, about 70,000 Tibetans had starved to death. Monasteries and temples were destroyed, and Tibetans could no longer worship freely.

Between 1950 and 1957, Mao's government had parceled off eastern Tibet into Chinese provinces. Most of Amdo became Qinghai Province, with the rest of it joining Gansu Province. Eastern Kham became part of Sichuan and Yunnan Provinces. On September 1, 1965, western Kham and the Tibetan provinces of Ü-Tsang and Ngari officially became the Tibet Autonomous Region (TAR).

In 1966, Mao started the Cultural Revolution, which was supposed to stamp out the "Four Olds": old thinking, old culture, old habits, and old customs. The goals of the revolution were carried out throughout China, including Tibet. By the time the Cultural Revolution ended in 1976 with Mao's death, Tibet was a sorry sight. Some estimates state that a million Tibetans had died from torture, execution, or starvation. Another hundred thousand, mainly Buddhist nuns and monks, were in prisons or labor camps. They had refused to denounce the Dalai Lama as a traitor. All but a handful of Tibet's more than 6,000 monasteries had been destroyed. Art treasures had been smashed or shipped to other parts of China. Farmers' and nomads' lands and animals belonged to the government, which told the farmers and nomads what, when, and how much to plant. Most of Tibet's forests had been chopped down, with the lumber sent to China.

China's new leaders realized that grave errors had been made, especially in Tibet. In 1978 and into the 1980s, the Chinese government reversed its earlier policies. Land was parcelled out to farmers, who could again grow their traditional barley crop. Some religious freedom was allowed. Tibetans started rebuilding monasteries and temples. Tibet was opened to tourists. However, during these same years the government encouraged thousands of Han Chinese to move to Tibet. They were given good jobs, high salaries, and interest-free loans. Soon Tibet's cities had more Han Chinese than Tibetans.

During the 1970s and 1980s, the Dalai Lama's government-in-exile kept the world informed about the plight of the Tibetans. In September 1987 the Dalai Lama addressed the U.S. Congressional Human Rights Caucus. He put forth a five-point peace plan for Tibet that called for establishing Tibet as a "Zone of Peace," stopping the immigration of Han Chinese, returning basic human rights and democratic freedoms to the Tibetans, protecting Tibet's natural environment, and holding talks between Tibet and China to plan Tibet's future. A few days later Tibetan monks in Lhasa held pro-independence rallies, which resulted in many arrests and deaths. In March 1988, more demonstrations led to more arrests and deaths. In June, in an address to the European Parliament, the Dalai Lama stated that he no longer sought independence for Tibet. Instead, he wanted true autonomy for Tibet, with China taking care of defense and foreign affairs. The U.S. Congress, the European Parliament, and the

Tibetans riot during the thirtieth anniversary of the 1959 Lhasa uprising.

parliaments of several countries have passed resolutions supporting the Dalai Lama's peace plans. China, however, has refused to begin talks.

On March 10, 1989, to mark the thirtieth anniversary of the Lhasa uprising, Tibetans held demonstrations in Lhasa that turned into riots. Chinese soldiers killed several Tibetans, arrested thousands more, and executed about 2,000 prisoners. Tibet was placed under martial law, and the Tibetans again lost many freedoms. The United States and many other countries condemned the Chinese treatment of Tibetans. In December 1989, the Dalai Lama was awarded the Nobel Peace Prize for his nonviolent approach for solving Tibet's problems.

In 1990, China lifted martial law, but pro-independence demonstrations continued throughout the 1990s. In 1996,

Tibetans set off bombs near Chinese government offices in Tibet. In that year, the Chinese government began a new campaign against religion in Tibet. It forbade the display of pictures of the Dalai Lama, encouraged people to denounce Buddhism, and placed undercover police in monasteries as spies.

Since 1991, the Dalai Lama has met with each U.S. president, who in turn has encouraged China's leaders to begin discussions for solving the Tibet question. The Chinese, however, continue to refuse. In 1997, the Dalai Lama stated that his reincarnation will not be born in Tibet if true autonomy and self-determination have not been established. In the meantime, hundreds of Tibetans continue to leave Tibet each year. In 2000, the leader of the Karmapa order escaped from his monastery and fled to Dharamsala, India. These Tibetans seek freedom with the Dalai Lama in Dharamsala, or in democratic countries in Europe and North America.

China's leaders seem willing to wait. When the current Dalai Lama dies, China may choose the Fifteenth Dalai Lama and force him on the Tibetan people. Meanwhile, more Han Chinese enter Tibet each year, further establishing Chinese Communist culture. Some political observers think that China is waiting until the Han Chinese eventually become the majority in Tibet. With a Han majority, the Chinese language would become the official language. Tibetans would then have an even harder time holding on to their own culture. At that point, as far as the Chinese are concerned, the Tibet question would be resolved.

A Region with Little Freedom

ECAUSE TIBET IS PART OF THE PEOPLE'S REPUBLIC OF China, the various levels of government in Tibet are considered local governments. When the Tibet Autonomous Region (TAR) was established in 1965, Tibet was divided into six prefectures and one municipality. Lhasa, the municipality, is also the capital of TAR. The prefectures are Chamdo, Lhoka, Nagchu, Ngari, Nyingtri, and Shigatse. Each prefecture has a capital.

The prefectures and municipality are divided into seventy-eight counties. Counties are further divided into numerous townships.

Prefectures and Municipality of TAR

1	Chamdo	**4**	Nagchu	**7**	Shigatse
2	Lhasa	**5**	Ngari	o	Administrative seat of prefecture
3	Lhoka	**6**	Nyingtri		

Lhasa: Did You Know This?

The word *lhasa* means "seat of the gods." Tibetans all over the world regard Lhasa as their holy city. About A.D. 640, Songtsen Gampo founded Lhasa as the capital of the Tibetan Empire. Before that time, the area was called *Rasa*, meaning "city of goats." Songtsen Gampo had the Jokhang and Ramoche Temples built and began building the Potala Palace. In the 1400s, the great monasteries of Ganden, Drepung, and Sera were built just outside the city. In the 1700s, the Dalai Lamas began building the Norbulingka, their summer palace.

Today thousands of Buddhist pilgrims come to Lhasa each year. On foot, they circle around the Jokhang Temple (above). Pilgrims pray in—and other visitors tour—the Potala Palace, which is now a museum. A public zoo is on the grounds of the Norbulingka Palace. The Chinese have put up many buildings made of concrete blocks. They often hide the few areas of traditional housing that still stand.

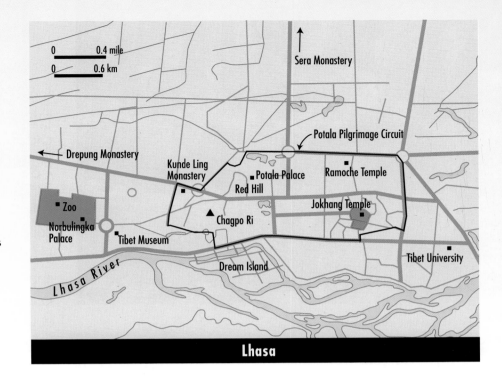

Population: 200,000

Location: On the Lhasa River

Founded: A.D. 600s

Average temperatures: 32°F (0°C) in January; 63°F (17°C) in July

Average annual precipitation: 57 inches (145 cm)

Lhasa

Governing Tibet

China's Constitution calls for the establishment of autonomous regions in areas where large numbers of people of one ethnic minority live. As an autonomous region of the People's Republic of China, Tibet is supposed to be self-governing. Governing bodies at the regional, prefectural, and county levels are supposed to make laws for the areas under their control. The major governing bodies are the Regional People's Congress and its Standing Committee, the Prefectures' People's Congresses and their Standing Committees, and the Counties' People's Congresses and their Standing Committees.

The people's congresses are supposed to have control of the economy and the natural resources of their area. In addition,

Chinese leaders stand for their national anthem during the opening session of the National People's Congress in Beijing.

local governments are supposed to control education, culture, public health, and security in their areas. However, before a regulation of a county or prefecture goes into effect, it must be approved by the Regional People's Congress Standing Committee. Furthermore, laws passed by the Regional People's Congress must be approved by the National People's Congress Standing Committee in Beijing, China. In reality, most laws are passed down from the Chinese government in Beijing. Tibet's government simply acts as a rubber stamp for the Chinese government.

The chairman and the vice chairman of the people's congresses and of the standing committees at all three local levels are supposed to be Tibetan, as is the head of the government. For the most part, these offices have been filled by Tibetans. Likewise, representation in the people's congresses at the regional, prefectural, and county levels is based on the size of ethnic groups. In elections to the Tibet Autonomous Regional People's Congress from 1965 to 1993, about 80 percent of

PARTS OF TIBET AUTONOMOUS REGION'S GOVERNMENT

REGIONAL PEOPLE'S CONGRESS

STANDING COMMITTEE OF REGIONAL PEOPLE'S CONGRESS

GOVERNMENT OF TIBET AUTONOMOUS REGION

the deputies were Tibetan. Many Tibetans also hold positions in the day-to-day operation of the government at various levels. However, these numbers tell only part of the story.

The Communist Party in Tibet

The real power in Tibet is controlled by the Central Committee of the Communist Party of China (CCCPC) in Beijing. The CCCPC appoints the secretary of the Communist Party in Tibet. In 2000, the CCCPC appointed Jin Long Guo, a Han Chinese, as secretary. As such, he is also head of the government in Tibet. Although Tibetans have served as vice secretaries of the Communist Party, they have never held the powerful post of secretary.

The Central Committee of the Communist Party of China holds talks with the CCCP of Vietnam.

In addition, for every Tibetan who holds a position in the day-to-day government, a Han Chinese Communist in a lesser position actually wields the power. In fact, the Chinese government continues to transfer Han Chinese Communists to Tibet to run the government.

One of China's goals for Tibet is to increase membership in the Communist Party. Individual members of the party are

China's army, the PLA, is a large force within Tibet.

A military checkpoint along a highway stops people from leaving Tibet.

called *cadres*. This term also applies to groups of party members who are active in recruiting new members. According to Chinese statistics, there were about 787,000 individual cadres in Tibet in 1998. Ethnic Tibetans made up about 72 percent of that number.

The Communist Party also controls China's army, the People's Liberation Army (PLA). Various estimates have placed the number of permanent Chinese troops in Tibet at 300,000 to more than 500,000. Tibetans are drafted into the PLA. The PLA commander's local headquarters is in Lhasa. Military bases practically encircle Tibet's largest cities, as a threat to political demonstrators. Chinese air bases have been built near Shigatse and Lhasa. Nuclear missile bases stand in eastern Tibet. To prevent people from leaving Tibet, military checkpoints have been set up along Tibet's southern border.

Human Rights and Political Prisoners

The Chinese Constitution states that all Chinese citizens, including those in autonomous regions, are guaranteed freedom of religion, speech, the press, association, assembly, and demonstration. According to the Constitution, they also have freedom from unlawful arrest and from false charges.

When Tibetans try to exercise their freedoms, however, they are usually arrested. About 450 Tibetans are now held in prisons and detention centers in Tibet. Monks and nuns make up about 73 percent of that number. Their crimes include taking part in pro-independence demonstrations, displaying photos of the Dalai Lama, and carrying the Tibetan flag. The Chinese government classifies these actions as "plotting to overthrow the

Demonstrators demand the release of the Eleventh Panchen Lama in 2001.

state" or "disturbing public order." Worse than being arrested is the treatment they receive in prison. Many are beaten and tortured. Most receive unfair trials if they receive a trial at all. Usually they're simply thrown in prison or placed in a labor camp.

Another human right that is frequently violated is a married couple's choice to have children. At first, the Chinese did not apply

RELEASE
The Youngest Prisoner of The World

RELEASE PANCHEN LAMA

family-size policies to the Tibetans. Now they do. Tibetans in cities are not supposed to have more than one child. Rural Tibetans are not allowed more than two or three.

Tibet's Flags

The national flag of the People's Republic of China (below) is the only flag that can be legally displayed in Tibet. It has a red background with five yellow stars. The red background stands for revolution; the large star represents China's Communist Party; and the four small stars symbolize the ethnic groups of the Chinese people, including the Tibetans.

Displaying the Tibetan national flag (right) is a crime. Tibetans have been shot or imprisoned for carrying it. The Thirteenth Dalai Lama designed the flag. He based it on Tibetan military flags that went back to those used by Songtsen Gampo. The white triangle stands for Tibet's snow-clad mountains; the sun and its rays represent the freedom, happiness, and prosperity to be enjoyed by all Tibetans; the six red bands stand for the legendary six tribes of Tibet; and the six blue bands represent the sky. Two snow lions, representing the unification of secular and spiritual life in Tibet, hold up a three-colored jewel that stands for the Three Supreme Jewels of Buddhism. Between their lower paws, the snow lions hold a two-colored swirling jewel that represents how the Tibetan people guard and cherish correct ethical behavior. The yellow border on three sides represents the spread of Buddhism. The white border shows that Tibet is also open to other religions.

To enforce these regulations, women are forced to have abortions or to be sterilized.

The United Nations and the legislatures of countries throughout the world have passed resolutions against China's human rights violations in Tibet. The Chinese government shows no signs of changing its policies. However, just before an important meeting with a world leader, China usually releases an important Tibetan political prisoner. In 2002 the abbot of Tashilhunpo and a music student were released from prison a few weeks before U.S. president George W. Bush met with the president of China in Beijing. The official policy of the United States is that Tibet is part of the People's Republic of China. U.S. presidents and diplomats, however, urge the Chinese to preserve Tibet's traditional culture and to protect the Tibetans' basic human rights.

National Anthem

The only national anthem that can be played or sung in Tibet is "March of the Volunteers," the anthem of the People's Republic of China. However, the Tibetans also have a national anthem that expresses their Buddhist beliefs of compassion and love and their hope for worldwide peace. Yongzin Trijang Rinpoche, a tutor to the Fourteenth Dalai Lama, wrote it.

The Tibetan National Anthem

Let the radiant light shine of Buddha's wish-fulfilling gem teachings,
the treasure mine of all hopes for happiness and benefit
in both worldly life and liberation.
O Protectors who hold the jewel of the teachings and all being,
nourishing them greatly,
may the sum of your virtuous deeds grow full.
Firmly enduring in a diamond-hard state, guard all directions with
Compassion and love.
Above our heads may divinely appointed rule abide
endowed with a hundred benefits and let the power increase of
four-fold auspiciousness.
May a new golden age of happiness and bliss spread
throughout the three provinces of Tibet,
and the glory expand of religious-secular rule.
By the spread of Buddha's teachings in the ten directions,
may everyone throughout the world
enjoy the glories of happiness and peace.
In the battle against dark negative forces
may the auspicious sunshine of the teachings and beings of Tibet
and the brilliance of a myriad radiant prosperities
be ever triumphant.

A Changing
Economy

Before China took over Tibet in the 1950s, the Tibetans engaged in a traditional economy based on agriculture and barter trade. Farmers mainly grew barley and traded with nomads for their yak meat and hides. Luxury goods such as tea, sugar, rice, silk, porcelain, copper, and iron were imported from neighboring countries. In return, Tibet exported wool and animal skins, salt, and medicinal herbs to those countries. For centuries Tibetans maintained a delicate balance between themselves and the environment. They kept the population low. They grew crops that thrived in cold weather and at high altitudes. They took care of the land. In return, the land provided well for them.

The Chinese, however, looked at the traditional economy as backward and in need of modernization. They also viewed Tibet as a vast wasteland to be developed by the Chinese for the good of China. Its forests and minerals would provide raw materials for Chinese industries, as well as goods to trade with other countries. Tibet's farmland and pastureland would provide food for China's large population. In addition, Tibet would provide homes for vast numbers of Han Chinese. Although the Chinese have spent billions of dollars trying to develop and modernize Tibet, they failed to take into account Tibet's climate, high altitudes, and natural environment.

Opposite: **People harvest barley in the fields outside Lhasa.**

Farmers begin spring planting

Agriculture

Between 1959 and the late 1970s, the Chinese government changed Tibet's agricultural system just as it was doing in the rest of China. The Chinese government took over some farmland as *state farms*. Farmers on state farms became employees who received a salary. Other farms were collectivized—that is, farmers were forced to pool their land, farm animals, and equipment and to work the land in common. These were called *collective farms*. The Tibetans were then forced to grow wheat and rice instead of barley. These crops do not grow well in Tibet's high altitudes and cool climate. Besides, the crops were planted year after year on the same land. This way of farming soon used up the nutrients in the soil.

The way of life for Tibet's nomads also changed. No longer could nomads move their herds of yaks, sheep, goats, and cattle to different grasslands throughout the year. They were forced to fence off pastureland into *communes*. The communes' pastures were too small for the size of the herds. Grazing in the same pastures throughout the year, the herds killed the grasses. In addition, nomads were also forced to plant crops on what had been pastureland.

As a result of China's agricultural policies, crop production dropped, thousands of head of livestock died, and hundreds of thousands of Tibetans starved to death. By the 1980s, China ended the commune system. Farmers and nomads were allowed to use more traditional methods. In 2002, Tibet's regional government planned to begin turning some farmland back into pastures and forests.

Workers in fields of barley, Tibet's leading crop.

Today, about 73 percent of Tibetans are farmers. They grow a variety of food crops and practice crop rotation. Barley once again leads the list. Other crops include wheat, soybeans, maize, millet, sorghum, buckwheat, rice, and rapeseed. Tibet's grain crops have some of the highest yields per acre in the world when compared to other countries with the same climate.

Tibet's 3,000 hours of sunshine each year help vegetables grow well. Sometimes cabbages grow as large as 26 pounds (12 kg), and a potato could weigh 1 pound (0.45 kg). Many other vegetables also grow well in Tibet. They include carrots, cauliflower, celery, kidney beans, lettuce, peas, radishes, spinach, squash, tomatoes, and turnips. Tibet's abundant sunshine allows some farmers to grow vegetables year-round in greenhouses. This is especially true near Lhasa. Large crops of fruits and nuts add even more variety to Tibetans' diets. They include apples, apricots, peaches, pears, chestnuts, and walnuts. Tea is now grown in parts of Nyingtri Prefecture.

About 15 percent of Tibetans are nomads, who herd about 21 million head of livestock on Tibet's 32 million acres (13 million ha) of pastureland. Their herds include yaks, goats, sheep, and cattle. They also raise horses, ponies, donkeys, and mules. In 2000, Tibet's livestock produced about 15,000 tons (13,500 metric tons) of meat, 17,000 tons (15,300 t) of milk, 8,000 tons (7,200 t) of sheep's wool, 1,500 tons (1,350 t) of goat's wool, and 600 tons (540 t) of cashmere. Because the price for cashmere has increased, more herders are raising the goats whose undercoats produce this special wool.

Nomads herding goats

Tibet's Yaks

About 30 percent of the world's domesticated yaks live in Tibet. These animals have three times as many oxygen-carrying red blood cells as regular cattle. Their thick, coarse outer coats cover a soft, woolly undercoat. These physical characteristics make the yak the perfect work animal in Tibet's high altitudes and cold climate. Nomads and traders use them to carry loads up to 154 pounds (70 kg). Farmers hitch them to plows to till the fields. Tibetans use all parts of the yak. They weave yak hair into ropes. Nomads spin the yaks' wool into felt to make bags, blankets, and tents. Milk from female yaks is made into cheese and butter. Yak dung

is collected, dried, and then used to fuel fires for cooking and heating. When a yak is killed, its hide is used for boot leather, and its heart and horns are used in Tibetan medicine. Yak meat is salted and dried into a kind of jerky.

What Tibet Grows, Makes, and Mines

Agriculture (2001 est.)

Barley	569,996 metric tons
Wheat	258,042 metric tons
Soybeans (1996 est.)	41,000 metric tons

Manufacturing (1990 est.)

Cement	132,300 metric tons
Vegetable oil	1,900 metric tons
Salt	1,000 metric tons

Mining (2000 est.)

Boromagnesite	16,000 metric tons
Tinkalite	1,500 metric tons
Chromite	11 metric tons

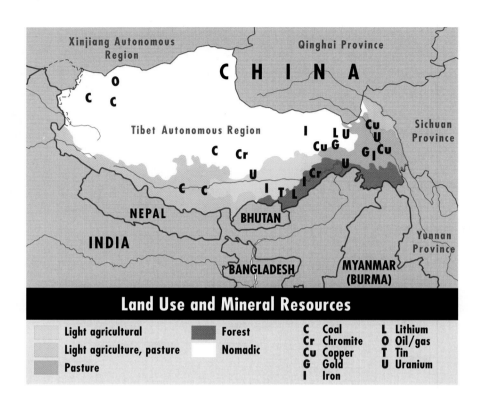

Land Use and Mineral Resources

Light agricultural	Forest
Light agriculture, pasture	Nomadic
Pasture	

C Coal
Cr Chromite
Cu Copper
G Gold
I Iron

L Lithium
O Oil/gas
T Tin
U Uranium

Manufacturing

Before 1950, Tibet had no mechanized industries. By the year 2000, Tibet had about 260 medium- and small-sized factories. They are owned by the Chinese government and employ about 51,000 workers. This is only about 2 percent of Tibet's population. Most factory workers, especially supervisors and managers, are Han Chinese.

Some of Tibet's largest industries, such as food processing and textiles, are based on farm products. For example, each year the Nyingtri Woolen Mill turns 1,250 tons (1,125 t) of wool into fabrics and carpets. Tanneries in Tibet's major cities

Tibetan women weave dyed wool into carpets at a rug factory in Lhasa.

process hides to produce leather shoes, jackets, and harnesses for horses. Breweries in cities process grains into a variety of Chinese and Tibetan beers. Other factories turn out about 300,000 tons (270,000 t) of cement each year. This material is greatly needed to build government offices and apartment buildings in Tibet's cities as more and more Han Chinese move into the region. Unfortunately, many of these industries cause air, ground, and water pollution, and the Chinese government is lax in enforcing antipollution requirements.

Tourism

Tourism has become one of Tibet's major industries. In 2001 tourism generated U.S.$82 million in Tibet from about 659,000 tourists and mountain climbers. To earn tourism dollars, the Chinese authorities have opened monasteries and temples to visitors and encourage monks to demonstrate Buddhist rituals. China also encourages the manufacture of traditional Tibetan handicrafts for the tourist trade.

The Chinese have even "found" the legendary Shangri-La. An area of southeastern TAR and Tibetan prefectures in Sichuan and Yunnan Provinces was renamed "The China Shangri-La Ecological Tourist Zone." This new attraction will bring in even more tourists.

Tourists, who bring more than $80 million a year to Tibet, explore central Tibet.

Currency

During its period of independence Tibet's government issued paper notes and coins. From 1912 to 1941 Tibetan banknotes called *tams* were printed in 5-, 10-, 15-, 25-, and 50-tam denominations. Between 1937 and 1959 notes called *srangs* were issued in denominations of 5, 10, 25, and 100, with 1 srang equal to 6.6 tam. Both tam and srang notes are known for their artistic designs. On the front of most notes the central design included a snow lion or pair of snow lions in various poses. The back of the notes had various designs that included outdoor scenes with mountains, flowers, waterfalls, animals, and a seated wise man, or Buddha. Buddhist symbols also appeared on the back of notes.

The currency of the People's Republic of China, *renminbi* ("people's money"), is now the only legal tender of Tibet. The unit of currency is the *yuan* (Y), which is divided into 10 *jiao*. The jiao is further divided into 10 *fen*. Paper notes are issued for 1, 2, and 5 jiao, and

for 2, 5, 10, 50, and 100 yuan. Coins are issued in denominations of 1 yuan; 5 jiao; and 1, 2, and 5 fen. In March 2003 8.28 yuan equaled U.S.$1. This rate of exchange has remained steady for several years.

The 50 Y note (above) combines China's and Tibet's histories. A picture of Mao Zedong is on the front of the note; the Potala Palace is on the back.

Mining and Energy

Mining is Tibet's single largest industry. Chinese reports state that Tibet has proven deposits of 126 minerals, including lithium, chromite, gold, silver, copper, iron, borax, zinc, and uranium. At least 120 mines are in operation throughout Tibet. One mine on the Chang Tang is supposed to have 50 percent of the world's lithium. In 2001, Chinese researchers reported

What a Yuan Can Buy in a Lhasa Restaurant

Item	Cost in Yuan	Cost in U.S.$
Apple tart	5 Y	$0.60
Bowl of yogurt	5 Y	0.60
Fruit salad	12.5 Y	1.50
Tsampa porridge with banana	15 Y	1.80
Yak burger with fries	45 Y	5.43

finding new oil and gas deposits that could total more than 5.5 billion tons (5 billion t). The Lhoka Chromite Mine and Norbusa Chromite Mine make chromite production a leading mining product.

Tibet's energy sources—water, sun, and wind—are almost limitless. Because its rivers have such steep drops in elevation, Tibet's waterpower for producing electricity is the highest in the world. The Thirteenth Dalai Lama built Tibet's first hydroelectric power plant near Lhasa. Since 1950, the Chinese have built several more throughout the region. The completion of the one at Yamdrok Tso has been delayed because a major tunnel for carrying water collapsed. The electricity from these power plants mainly benefits factories, businesses, and homes in cities.

Tibet's hot springs and geysers are underground sources of water energy. The Yangpachen Geothermal Plant already supplies Lhasa with electricity. If these sources in western and northern Tibet were tapped into, electricity could reach farmers and nomads in those areas. Solar power is another energy source. Tibet's high altitude brings it closer than any other part of the world to the sun's power. Only the Sahara Desert in Africa has greater potential for developing solar energy. For some time, solar ovens on rooftops in Lhasa have been used for cooking. In 2002, Chinese reports stated that solar energy powered washing machines, radios, and televisions in rural Tibet. The strong winds that blow year-round across the Chang Tang are another source of electrical power that could benefit rural Tibetans. So far, only experimental wind power stations have been built there.

Solar heat collectors on rooftops of Tibetan homes convert enough energy to power televisions and radios.

Transportation and Communication

In 1950, three cars that belonged to the Dalai Lama were the only vehicles with wheels in Tibet. The British had given them to the Thirteenth Dalai Lama. However, there were no real roads on which to drive them. Tibetans did not even use carts or wheelbarrows. Today, Tibet has 13,670 miles (22,000 km) of highways, not all of which are paved. They were built by PLA soldiers and by the forced labor of Tibetan prisoners and other Tibetans. Four highways link Tibet to its neighboring Chinese provinces and autonomous regions. The China-Nepal Friendship Highway connects Lhasa to Nepal's capital, Kathmandu. Although there are about 30,000 cars and trucks in Tibet, most

Horse-drawn carts travel along the Friendship Highway.

Bicycles are the main form of transportation for most Tibetans.

Tibetans get around by walking or bicycling.

In 2001 work began on Tibet's first railroad. When it is completed, the railroad will run from Lhasa to Golmud in the Qinghai Province of China. It will be the highest railroad in the world. Many Tibetans fear that the railroad, like the highways, will simply make it easier for more Han Chinese to move to Tibet and for more of Tibet's mineral and forest products to leave.

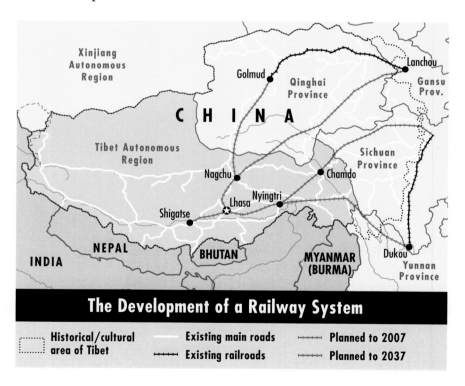

The Development of a Railway System

······ Historical/cultural area of Tibet   —— Existing main roads   +–+–+ Planned to 2007

+–+–+ Existing railroads   +–+–+ Planned to 2037

When Bamda Airport in Chamdo was completed in 1994, Tibet gained a second airport for commercial flights. Before that, Tibet's only airport for passengers was Gonggar, outside of Lhasa.

Various forms of communication offer links within Tibet as well as to the outside world. Tibet has fifteen newspapers and thirty-six periodicals. The *Tibet Daily* is the region's major newspaper, with both a Chinese and a Tibetan edition. An important periodical is *Tibetan Literature and Arts*. Tibet also has two radio stations and two television stations. Much radio programming is in Tibetan. Tibet TV Station broadcasts in Chinese, while Lhasa Station has some programs in Tibetan.

By 1999, seventy-four of Tibet's seventy-eight counties had telephone service. Most phones are in businesses, government offices, and hotels. In 2000, about 57,000 people had cell phones. Computers and the Internet have also made inroads in Tibet. By 2002, more than 4,000 people were registered Internet users. Most computers with Internet capabilities are in Internet cafés, bars, and restaurants.

A Tibetan woman checks her e-mail at an Internet café.

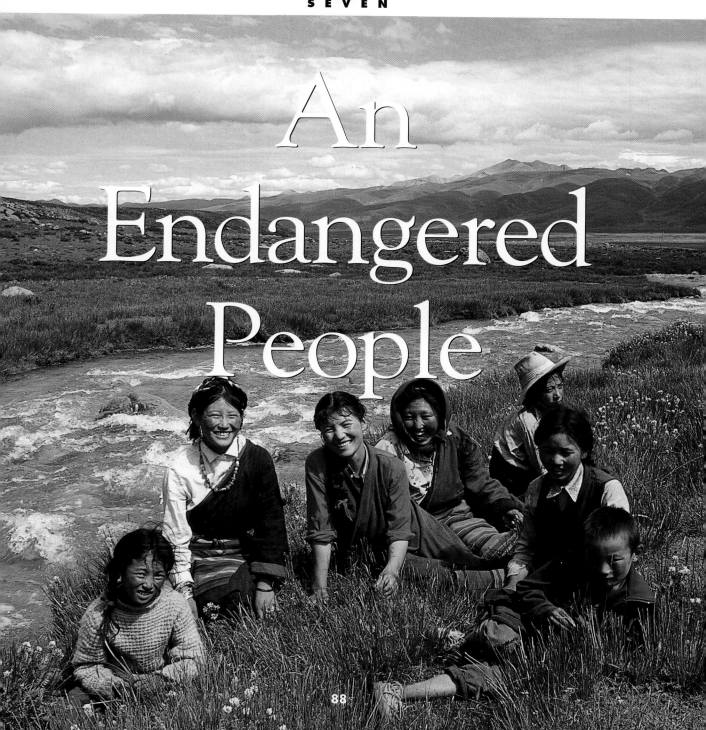

An Endangered People

According to China's census in 2001, Tibet had a total population of 2,620,000. This makes its population the smallest of all China's provinces and regions. The state of Kansas in the United States has about the same number of people. Tibet has a low population density: about five people per square mile (two per sq km). However, about 85 percent of Tibet's people live in the southern Yarlung Tsangpo Riber valley and the eastern valleys and forestlands. Most of these people live in villages and work as farmers. Other people in southern and eastern Tibet live and work in or near the region's major cities.

About 15 percent of the population live in western Tibet and along the southern edge of the Chang Tang. No one lives in the northern Chang Tang or at the highest altitudes of Tibet's many mountains.

Opposite: **A group of young Tibetan nomads**

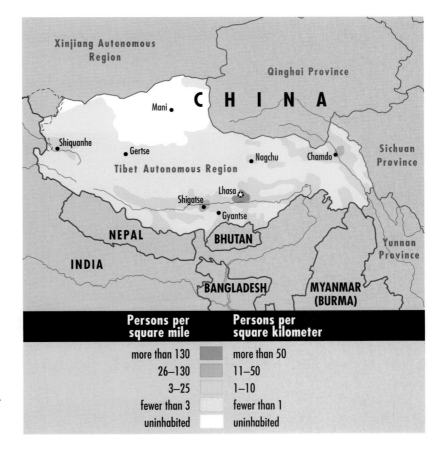

Persons per square mile / Persons per square kilometer

Persons per square mile		Persons per square kilometer
more than 130		more than 50
26–130		11–50
3–25		1–10
fewer than 3		fewer than 1
uninhabited		uninhabited

**Population of
Major Cities**

Lhasa	200,000
Shigatse	60,000
Tsetang	25,000
Gyantse	15,000

The People of Tibet

China's census for 2000 states that Tibetans make up 92.2 percent of TAR's population; Han Chinese, 5.9 percent; and other ethnic groups, 1.9 percent. Tibet's government-in-exile, however, claims that more Chinese than Tibetans are now living in Tibet. Some of these Chinese are PLA soldiers and government officials who are counted in their home census area rather than in Tibet's. A census conducted by a neutral group, such as the United Nations, might be the only way to resolve this dispute. There is no disputing the fact, however, that Han Chinese make up the majority of Lhasa's population. Government representatives and tourists alike have observed this. In addition, the great amount of building construction under way in all of Tibet's cities is mainly for the Han Chinese.

**A fruit stand in the Chinese
section of Tsetang, Tibet**

The other major non-Tibetan ethnic groups in Tibet are the Monpa and the Lohpa. About 7,000 Monpa live in southeastern Tibet, mainly in Nyingtri Prefecture. Most of them are farmers whose crops include rice, corn, buckwheat, and millet. These crops form the basis of their diet. The Monpa speak and write Tibetan, and most practice Buddhism. The Lohpa number about 2,000 and live in Lhoka and Nyingtri Prefectures. They are also farmers whose staple foods are corn, millet, rice, and buckwheat. Each of these groups has a distinctive type of dress that includes headgear and jewelry.

A Monpa woman and child

Tibetans Outside TAR

When China divided Tibet in the 1950s, the Tibetan people were split apart. Today, about 2.5 million Tibetans live in Qinghai, Gansu, Sichuan, and Yunnan Provinces of China. In these provinces, they are definitely in the minority. Because the Tibetans in China are separated geographically and have become or are becoming the minority groups there, they find it hard to hold on to their language, religion, and culture.

In Qinghai Province, China, crowds watch a display at a Tibetan festival.

Tibetan orphans attend school at the Tibetan Children's Village in Dharamsala, India.

More than 100,000 Tibetans live outside China. Most of them live in nearby India, Nepal, and Bhutan. The Dalai Lama heads the government-in-exile in Dharamsala, which is in northwestern India. His democratic-style government, based on a 1962 constitution, has an elected legislature, a Supreme Justice Commission, and all the departments that any government would have.

The Tibetan Children's Village in Dharamsala is a home and school for Tibetan orphans. Other children have been smuggled out of Tibet and sent to Dharamsala so that they will receive a traditional Tibetan education and not be forced to learn Chinese. In southern India Tibetan monks have set up new Drepung, Ganden, and Sera Monasteries, naming them for their monasteries in Tibet.

Other Tibetans have settled in the United States, Canada, Australia, England, France, Switzerland, and other countries. Although most of these refugees continue to work to restore human rights and self-government in Tibet, they are also self-supporting members of their new communities.

Tibetans are generally a healthy, hardy, and slim people. Their blood is unlike that of any other people on earth. Over the centuries, Tibetans' bodies have adapted to life at high altitudes. Because the air at high altitudes has less oxygen, Tibetans' bodies need more hemoglobin—the oxygen-carrying part of the blood. In fact, they have 20 percent more of these oxygen carriers than do people living at lower altitudes. When tourists come to Tibet, it takes them several days to get used to the air at the high altitudes. For this reason, an oxygen tank is standard equipment in Tibet's hotel rooms. Also, at high altitudes the body burns more calories. This keeps Tibetans slim and healthy.

A Tibetan medicine man who practices in the traditional way, feels the pulse of this woman.

When Tibetans do get sick, they prefer to see Tibetan doctors who practice traditional Tibetan medicine. According to this medicine, the body is kept in balance by certain forces. Sickness results from an imbalance in these forces. Traditional doctors determine the cause of the imbalances by feeling the pulse. The usual treatment is a prescription of medicine made from one or more of Tibet's 2,000 medicinal plants, parts of animals, and maybe even rocks. Other treatments might include massage with medicinal oils for nerve or muscle diseases. Baths in natural spring waters are prescribed for skin diseases.

In recent years, the health of Tibetans has been declining. Some of this is caused by air, water, and ground pollution. Pneumonia and tuberculosis are on the rise. Tibet's rate of tuberculosis is twice as high as the rest of China's. Tibetan children are suffering from malnutrition. This shows up in low height for their age, poor brain development, and a bone disease known as rickets. The death rates for children and adults in Tibet are two to three times higher than in the rest of China. Life expectancy in Tibet is sixty-five years; in the rest of China, it is seventy-one years.

The Tibetan Language

A sign in Chinese and English

Tibetans' identity as a people is held together by their language. Tibetan and Mandarin Chinese are both official languages in Tibet. However, it is becoming harder for Tibetans to succeed unless they know Chinese, a language that has nothing in common with Tibetan. Chinese is the official language for business and government. To get a good job in an office, a factory, or the government, Tibetans must speak and read Chinese. Chinese is also becoming the official language in Tibet's schools. Even in elementary school all lessons are taught in

Chinese, so Tibetan children do not have the chance to learn their own written language. Children in rural areas where lessons are still taught in Tibetan will not find work in Tibet's cities without Chinese. As more and more Tibetans took part in protests during the 1990s, China also identified the Tibetan language with the people. By forcing the Chinese language on Tibetans, China hopes they will lose their cultural identity and no longer cause problems.

The Tibetan language is part of the Tibetan-Burman language group, which in turn is part of the Sino-Tibetan language family. Over many centuries, various dialects of

Though Mandarin Chinese must be learned by Tibetans, using the Tibetan language helps them retain their culture.

Tibetan developed. Today they are heard throughout Tibet as well as among Tibetans in other parts of China and in India, Nepal, and Bhutan. The dialect spoken in Lhasa, however, is understood by most Tibetans. Spoken Tibetan uses falling and rising tones. Unlike in English, questions end in a falling tone. Also, Tibetan sentences follow subject-object-verb order. For example, "I walked home" would be "I home walked" in Tibetan.

Written Tibetan is the same no matter what the spoken dialect. The Tibetan alphabet has thirty consonants, including *a*, and four vowels: *e*, *i*, *o*, and *u*. Like the English alphabet, this alphabet represents sounds. The Tibetan alphabet and its script are based on an early Indian script. As a result, these characters do not translate easily into English and a Tibetan word might have several English spellings.

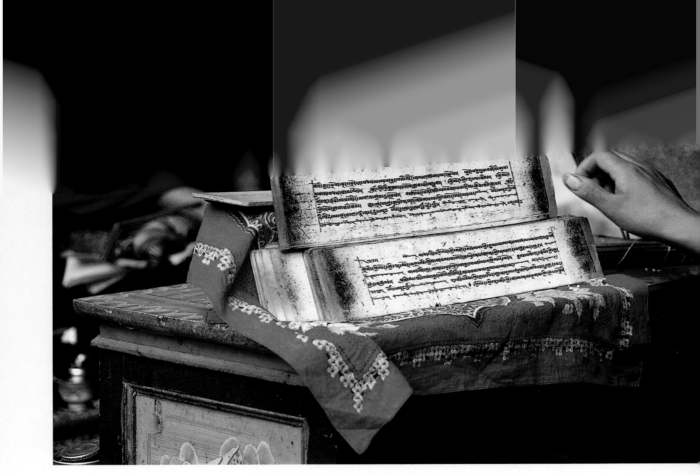

Tibetan Writing Styles

There are four ways of writing Tibetan. Only capital letters are used for newspapers, books, and other printed material.

Buddhist texts and scriptures have their own style (above). A decorative cursive script is used for formal writing. An informal script is used for everyday writing.

Tibetans' Names

A few days after a baby is born, parents take it to a lama to receive a name. Sometimes the lama writes down a secret name and puts the paper in a small bag that the child wears around his or her neck forever.

Lamas also give babies the names they will use throughout their lives. They might be named after a day of the week or a month of the year. There is no clear distinction between names for boys and those for girls. For example, *Jigme* is both a male and a female name. Children don't necessarily have the same last name as either their father or their mother. To add to the confusion, one person's first name might be another's last name.

A Spiritual Land

Between 1959 and the late 1970s, Chinese policy was to wipe out religion from Tibet. Most of Tibet's 6,000 monasteries were destroyed. Other religious buildings such as temples were used as storerooms. Religious articles, sacred writings, and artwork were destroyed or carted off to China. Monks and nuns were forced to become laborers or were thrown into prison. Ordinary Tibetans could not openly practice their religion. However, Buddhism remained strong in Tibet.

In the 1980s, China reversed its policy somewhat to allow religion on a limited basis. The Chinese government claims to have spent about U.S.$50 million to rebuild, repair, and restore the Jokhang Temple and 1,787 monasteries. The monasteries include such major ones as Samye, Drepung, Sera, Ganden, and Tashilhunpo. They also claim to have provided gold, silver, and precious jewels to repair and replace the artwork that they destroyed. The labor for these repairs has been supplied by Tibetans, usually on a volunteer basis. Tibetans have also paid for much of

Opposite: **Religious items in Jokhang Temple in Lhasa**

Ganden Monastery was damaged during the Chinese Cultural Revolution and has only been partly repaired.

A Spiritual Land   **99**

Religions of Tibet	
Buddhism	2,400,000
Bon	unknown
Islam	2,000
Christianity	600

the repair work themselves. Tibetans are again allowed to become nuns and monks, but the Chinese government has limits on their number. If nuns or monks take part in political demonstrations and are arrested, they cannot go back to their monasteries.

Today, freedom of religion is still limited. Tibetans cannot display images of the Dalai Lama. Schoolchildren are warned not to go on pilgrimages or take part in religious celebrations during their school vacations. Older, retired people are threatened with loss of their government pension money if they are found in crowds during celebrations. In spite of these restrictions, Tibetans continue to practice their religion. According to the Chinese government, nearly all Tibetans are Tibetan Buddhists, about 600 Tibetans are Catholic, and about 2,000 Hui people follow Islam. An unknown number of Tibetans also practice the Bon religion.

A mural in a Bon temple depicts the god Chenrap.

The Bon Religion

The Bon religion developed first in western Tibet and was supported by the early Yarlung kings. Bonpo, the followers of Bon, divided the world into heaven, earth, and the underworld. They worshiped spirits who lived on mountaintops and in lakes. Bon priests performed rites and rituals based on magic and spells. They used their magic to control demons who lived in mountains, forests, and water. Bon priests presided over the funeral rites of the Yarlung kings. They sacrificed yaks or sheep and—sometimes even the kings' servants—so the king would be happy in the land of the dead.

By the 900s, Bon had come to resemble the more recently established religion of Buddhism. Bon became more organized, with temples and monasteries. Today, the major Bon monasteries are Menri and Yungdrung Ling, both near Shigatse. Sometimes it is difficult to tell apart Buddhists and Bonpo. One main difference is the way members of the two groups walk around a sacred site. Bonpo walk counterclockwise; Buddhists, clockwise.

A statue of the Buddha at the Potala Palace

Buddhism

Buddhism came to Tibet from India and China in the A.D. 600s. This religion's beliefs were founded by the Nepalese prince Siddhārtha Gautama about 528 B.C. Troubled by the problems of the world, he decided to find the cause of human suffering. After six years of thinking and meditating, he realized that people suffer because they desire life and things. When he reached this state of enlightenment, he became known as the Buddha, the Enlightened One. From then until his death in 483 B.C., he taught the Four Noble Truths and his Eightfold Path to enlightenment.

The Four Noble Truths are:
1. Life has many kinds of suffering.
2. Suffering is caused by a desire for life and for things.
3. Suffering ends when desire stops.
4. Desire will end by following the Eightfold Path.

Steps in the Eightfold Path are right understanding, right thought, right speech, right action, right livelihood, right effort, right mindfulness, and right concentration.

People who do not follow the Eightfold Path and do not become enlightened are reborn into another life until they achieve enlightenment. This is the Buddhist belief of *reincarnation*—birth, death, and rebirth. People can repeat this cycle of rebirth forever. A person's *karma*—the result of good or bad actions in his or her life—determines the type of life into which that person will be reborn. The goal of life for Buddhists is to reach *nirvana*. This is the state of enlightenment in which suffering and the cycle of rebirth ends. Some people who reach enlightenment decide to come back as a *bodhisattva*. Bodhisattvas help others reach enlightenment.

A lama of the Gelukpa order wearing traditional clothing holds objects used in religious rites.

Tibetan Buddhism

Although there are many bodhisattvas, Tibetans are devoted to Chenresi, the Bodhisattva of Compassion. Tara, the female Bodhisattva of Compassion, is Tibet's protective goddess. Tibetans believe that the Dalai Lamas are rebirths of the Bodhisattva Chenresi. The rebirth of lamas is central to Tibetan Buddhism. Lamas are monks who have reached a high state of wisdom and holiness. Before a lama dies, he can choose when and where he will be reborn. Following his death, a group of monks from his monastery begin the search for his reincarnation. Reincarnated lamas are sometimes called *Rinpoche*, which means "Precious One."

The Dalai Lama is Tibet's spiritual leader. The next lama in importance is the Panchen Lama. He is believed to be the reincarnation of the Buddha called *Amitabha*. The Tashilhunpo Monastery is the home base for the Panchen Lamas. Panchen Lamas are often important in finding Dalai Lamas' reincarnations.

The Eleventh Panchen Lama: The World's Youngest Political Prisoner

In 1989, the Tenth Panchen Lama died. In 1995 his reincarnation was identified by a search committee of senior lamas from Tashilhunpo Monastery. The Dalai Lama confirmed the identification of six-year-old Gedhun Choekyi Nyima as the Eleventh Panchen Lama. The Chinese government kidnapped the young boy and his parents and took them into custody in Beijing. The Chinese then selected six-year-old Gyaltsen Norbu (left) as the Panchen Lama and installed him in Tashilhunpo Monastery. Tibetans across the land protested. International agencies and human rights organizations have tried to visit Gedhun Choekyi Nyima and his family, but the Chinese have refused any outside contact with them. The International Campaign for Tibet is working for their freedom. They call this young boy the world's youngest political prisoner.

Another important aspect of Tibetan Buddhism is the idea that all is impermanent. That is, nothing lasts; everything eventually passes away. Through this belief, Tibetans face death as a natural part of life. They believe that after death they pass through a period called *bardo*. After this period of up to forty-nine days, they are reborn. During bardo, if a person realizes the true nature of reality, he or she is released from the cycle of rebirth and reaches nirvana.

Daily Practices of Tibetan Buddhists

Gaining merit during life is a way to achieve good karma and thus a better life in rebirth. Giving alms to the needy and helping others are ways of gaining merit. Prayer, chanting, and other forms of worship also gain merit.

Chanting mantras is a way for Buddhists to gain merit and achieve good karma.

The mantra *Om mani padme hum*—pronounced "ohm mah nee pahd may hum"—is chanted, or said over and over, by Tibetans. This is the mantra of the Bodhisattva Chenresi. The usual translation of this mantra is "Hail to the Jewel in the Lotus." Chenresi, like the Buddha, is seated on a lotus blossom and adorned with jewels.

Prayer flags lace the sky for the Tibetan New Year.

Om mani padme hum is often the mantra written on Tibet's colorful cotton prayer flags. Tibetans fly them from their roofs, between trees, and at mountain passes. The flags are arranged in a sequence of blue, white, red, green, and yellow. The colors stand for space, water, fire, air, and earth. The figure of a wind horse is usually in the center of the flag. Wind power takes the blessings of the prayer out into the world. New sets of flags are put out on the third day of the Tibetan New Year.

Pilgrims spin prayer wheels outside Jokhang Temple.

Tibetans also gain merit by turning prayer wheels. These bronze cylinders on a stick contain a prayer written on a piece of paper. The most common prayer in prayer wheels is also the mantra *Om mani padme hum*. Rows of large prayer wheels turned by waterpower line the outside walls of temples. Each time a person spins either kind of prayer wheel, the prayer is considered said.

Counting off prayers on a rosary is another way of praying. Tibetan rosaries have 108 beads. Tibetans keep track of the number of prayers said by marking off the beads. The number 108 is important to Tibetans because they believe 108 bodhisattvas are working for their welfare.

Pilgrims doing prostrations at Mount Kailash

Tibetan Buddhists try to go on pilgrimages to holy sites as often as possible. The two main destinations of pilgrims are the Jokhang Temple in Lhasa and Mount Kailash. At the holy site, the pilgrims practice circumambulation. That is, they walk around and around it—always in a clockwise direction. Tibetans believe that if they circumambulate Mount Kailash 108 times, they will achieve instant enlightenment.

Some pilgrims not only circumambulate, but they do it in *prostrations*. They stretch out on the ground, rise up, place their feet where their head just was, and stretch out to begin the process again. They do this the entire way around a holy site. Some Tibetans travel from their home to the holy site in a long series of prostrations, taking months to arrive.

Mani stones carved with a Buddhist mantra

Along the way and at holy sites, pilgrims leave piles of rocks called *mani* stones. On them, they carve or paint the mantra *Om mani padme hum*. This is another way of gaining merit.

Important Religious Holidays

Losar, Tibetan New Year	February
Monlam, the Great Prayer Festival	February or March
Sakadawa, the Birth of the Buddha	May
Chokor Duchen, the Buddha's First Teaching	July
Lhabab Duchen, the Buddha's Return to Earth	September
Festival of Lamps	December

Maintaining a Traditional Culture

EVEN AFTER MORE THAN FIFTY YEARS OF CHINA'S attempts to modernize Tibet, Tibetans' lives continue to revolve around their traditional culture. Birth, marriage, and funeral customs are carried out much as before. Families carry on making traditional arts and crafts. The Tibetans have worked hard to restore palaces, monasteries, temples, and chortens. They enjoy art, literature, and music that are more than a thousand years old.

Opposite: **A ninth-generation thanka painter keeps Tibetan culture alive.**

The Tibetan Calendar

Tibet uses a lunar calendar that was introduced in A.D. 1027. Each year astrologers figure out important dates for the new year. Tibetans don't know from one year to the next when holidays and festivals will fall. The lunar calendar is about one to two months behind the Western solar calendar.

Sky Burial

Tibetan Buddhists' beliefs in impermanence and living in harmony with the environment are expressed in the practice of sky burial. Tibetans believe that in death the soul leaves the body, making the body an empty shell. Because Tibetan Buddhists do not waste anything, they make a gift of their body to the birds. The dead person's body is taken to a special, high, rocky place outside of a city or town. *Domdens*, body breakers, then cut the body into pieces and pound the bones together with *tsampa*. Vultures, ravens, and other birds of prey carry off the pieces. Thus, the dead person is buried in the sky.

Most Tibetans are given a sky burial. Because wood to burn for cremations is so scarce, only lamas and senior monks are cremated. The bodies of young children are sometimes placed in rivers to provide food for fish. Only criminals and those who died from infectious diseases are buried in the ground.

Instead of counting years in groups of a hundred—a century—the Tibetan calendar is based on a cycle of sixty years. Each year has its own name based on a combination of twelve animals (hare, dragon, snake, horse, sheep, monkey, bird, dog, boar, mouse, bull, and tiger) and five elements (iron, water, wood, fire, and earth). Each sixty-year cycle starts with the year of the Fire Hare and ends with the Fire Tiger. The year 2002 was the Year of the Water Horse; 2003, the Water Sheep; and 2004, the Wood Monkey. The current cycle began in 1987 and will end in 2046.

Traditional Arts and Crafts

Tibetans continue their ancient crafts of carpet weaving and metalwork. Wool for the carpets comes from sheep on the Chang Tang. Their wool has a high lanolin content, which makes for a long-lasting carpet with a high sheen. Vegetable dyes provide more than thirty colors for the carpets' dragon, bird, and flower designs. Carpet sizes vary from those used on beds, called *kadens*, to those that cover the floor, called *sadens*. Metalworkers craft statues of the Buddha and other deities that are displayed in temples and in homes. They also make

Metalworkers creating Buddhist sculptures at the Tashilhunpo Monastery

Butter sculptures carved by Tibetan monks

other items used in Buddhist ceremonies, such as bells and *dorjes*, or thunderbolts.

Tibetan monks are known for their butter sculptures. On the fifteenth day of the Monlam Festival, monks carve huge statues from yak butter of the Buddha, flowers, and animals. The statues are painted and set in front of the Jokhang Temple, where pilgrims say prayers as they walk around them during the night. In the morning sun, the statues melt. This is an example of the Buddhist idea that all things are impermanent.

A sand mandala

Mandalas are another Tibetan Buddhist art form. These drawings are patterns of circles and squares with a deity, or supreme being, in the center. Mandalas appear as wall paintings in temples and monasteries. Monks also make mandalas, drawing the patterns with colored sand. They then stare at the mandala as they meditate until they become one with the deity. As another example of impermanence, the monks sweep up or blow away the sand when the meditation is over.

Thangkas are another famous kind of Tibetan Buddhist art. They are paintings of the Buddha or another deity done on cotton cloth that has a rod at the top. Thangkas are also used in meditation. They can be rolled up around the rod to be carried on pilgrimages. Some thangkas hang on walls of homes. Others are used in special ceremonies during festivals. These thangkas are so large that they cover a hillside or an entire outside wall of a monastery.

Architecture

Tibet developed a distinct style of architecture. Its traditional buildings have a broad base with inward-sloping walls. Because few trees grow in most of Tibet, stones and sunbaked bricks were the main building materials. The outside walls were whitewashed. A band of wood usually was placed between the top of the walls and the roof. The wooden trim was then painted in bright colors. Because Tibet receives little snow and rain, roofs on most buildings are flat. Small windows are placed high in the walls to receive sunshine but keep out Tibet's strong, cold winds. In large buildings, such as temples and monastery assembly halls, the roof is supported inside by rows of columns. Some of these buildings have 108 columns. The Potala Palace is a good example of this style of architecture.

The Potala Palace

The Potala Palace was first built in the mid-600s as the center for the court of the Yarlung kings. Chinese invaders burned down the original palace in the late 600s. The Red and White Palaces of the Potala were built during the reign of the Great Fifth Dalai Lama. Since then, it served as the home of the ruling Dalai Lamas. During the Chinese crackdown in 1959 and the Cultural Revolution (1966–1976), the Potala suffered some damage. Today, it is restored and open as a museum for Tibetans as well as foreign visitors. Its thirteen stories rise 383 feet (117 m). This huge monument has more than 1,000 rooms, about 10,000 shrines, and more than 200,000 paintings and statues of the Buddha, other deities, and Dalai Lamas. The Potala was built of wood and stone, and 8,000 artisans and builders constructed the Red Palace alone. This was all done without wheeled vehicles or machinery.

Kumbum Chorten

The Kumbum Chorten, or stupa, at Gyantse is another good example of Tibetan architecture. *Kumbum* means "100,000 images," and the chorten probably has that many statues and paintings of the Buddha and other deities in its seventy-seven chapels. This six-story shrine is Tibet's largest chorten. The first five levels represent earth, fire, water, air, and space. The pointed top of the chorten represents enlightenment. Other chortens are found throughout Tibet, as a part of a monastery or standing alone. Most of them house sacred texts or other holy relics. Some even have cremated remains of the bodies of lamas of other holy men.

Monastery and temple architecture is also special to Tibet. Most monasteries and temples are built like a huge three-dimensional mandala. A statue of the Buddha is usually in the middle of the main building. In monasteries, a central courtyard is used for special ceremonies and festivals. An outside wall protects the monastery from the outside world. Around the outside wall is a *kora*, a path for pilgrims to circumambulate. The flat roofs on monasteries provide a platform for monks to stand on as they blow their horns to call the community to prayer. Atop the roofs of Tibetan monasteries and temples stand three statues: the Wheel of Dharma, which represents the Buddhist way of life, and two deer—one on each side of the wheel. Deer were in the Indian garden where the Buddha first taught.

**Wheel of Dharma
and two deer**

Most early Tibetans could not read. In fact, many still do not know how to read today. These people relied on storytellers who walked from village to village reciting poems and stories. The epic poem *King Gesar of Ling* is the most famous of these stories. Made up of about 2 million verses, this is the world's longest epic poem. Gesar battled demons and evil kings to bring peace and justice to Tibet. Many think he was the king of mythical Shambhala, or Shangri-La, and that he will return with his army to bring peace and justice once more to Tibet. Eventually this epic was written down. It has been translated into many languages so people around the world can enjoy the story.

Most of Tibet's written literary heritage revolves around Buddhism. The first books were translations of important Buddhist works. The *Kangyur* is several volumes of the Buddha's teachings. The *Tengyur* is even more volumes of scholars' interpretations of the *Kangyur*. In the 1300s, the scholar Karmalingpa wrote *The Book of the Dead*. This work describes bardo, the stage that souls go through between death and

Milarepa: Saint and Scholar

Tibet's most famous poet is the Buddhist monk Milarepa (1040–1123). He came from a noble family whose fortune was stolen by his uncle. To gain back his family's land, Milarepa learned magic. With the magic, he killed his uncle's son and destroyed his uncle's crops. Because Milarepa was so sorry for what he had done, he left home. He wandered until he found a great teacher—Marpa, the founder of the Kagyupa order.

Marpa taught him how to meditate, and Milarepa became a great monk and holy man. Milarepa lived in caves in western and southern Tibet. There he wrote the poems that are known as *The Hundred Thousand Songs*. Because he lived such a good and holy life, Tibetans believe he achieved enlightenment in just one lifetime. Images of him show him smiling with his hand raised to his right ear.

rebirth. Monks wrote many other books, including stories or plays about battles between deities and demons, and biographies of Buddhist saints. Tibet does not have a history of fiction writing, even today.

Many of these early works were destroyed by the Communist government. Today, Tibetan scholars have to officially criticize these works. However, when the criticisms are published, Tibetans like to read them because so much of the old stories are retold.

Early Tibetan books, as well as many printed today, are works of art. Their pages are long, narrow, horizontal pieces of paper. Some were printed on printing presses; others, with separate woodblocks. Words were carved from a block of wood, the block was coated with ink, a piece of paper was pressed against the block to print the page. When all the pages had been printed, they were pressed together between two pieces of wood and then wrapped in a colorful piece of cloth.

Library of Buddhist texts in the Potala Palace

Tibet has a long history of religious and secular music and dance. The best-known religious music is chanting, which helps monks in their prayers. Through meditation, monks develop the special techniques used in Tibetan Buddhist chanting. As a result, a monk can "stack" notes on top of one another, singing two or three notes at the same time. This is like playing a chord on a piano. Some monks can reach the lowest tone of the human voice, sounding almost like a bass fiddle or the vibration of a bass drum.

Sometimes during chanting, monks use musical instruments, including bells and drums. They also have many kinds of horns, such as conch shells; *dungchen*, or long horns; *gyaling*, or silver scroll trumpets; and *kangling*, or thigh-bone trumpets. Thigh-bone trumpets are human bones coated with silver. Using human bones shows the impermanence of life.

Horns are one type of musical instrument played by monks.

Some of Tibet's earliest popular music was work songs. Tibet's serfs and farmers sang songs to give a rhythm to their work in the fields. Other music included love songs, wedding songs, drinking songs, and songs to accompany dances. Musicians accompanied these songs with the *dragnen*, the Tibetan lute, and the *gyumang*, a multistring dulcimer.

Tibet's most famous dances are the *cham* dances performed by monks at special festivals. Monk dancers wear colorful costumes and scary masks of animals or deities. The monks completely lose themselves to the mask they are wearing. Some dances last two or three days.

A Tibetan monk dancing in a fearsome mask

Daily Life and Special Occasions

TIBETANS HAVE WITNESSED MANY CHANGES IN THE PAST fifty years. However, many aspects of their daily life go on much as they did before. Tibetans eat many of the same foods and wear traditional clothing. They also celebrate holidays and festivals that have been observed for hundreds of years.

Tibetan Food

The staples of the Tibetan diet are *tsampa* (roasted barley flour), yak butter, and tea. Yak-butter tea is the main drink throughout Tibet. To make it, black tea is strained and mixed with yak butter and salt in a wooden churn before it is heated in a kettle. Tibetans drink many cups of this each day. They

Yak-butter tea, a major drink in Tibet, is poured from a thermos to a kettle outside Ganden Monastery.

carry colorful thermoses of it wherever they go. In the cool, dry, high-altitude climate, the tea warms them, adds moisture to their bodies, and supplies extra calories. Yak-butter tea is also mixed with tsampa to make a dough that is eaten by hand.

Nomads add to this basic diet yak meat and mutton, yogurt, and cheeses. The meats are cut into strips, dried, and eaten like jerky. One particularly hard cheese is sucked, almost like a candy. With Tibet's high altitude and cool climate, dairy foods and meats keep unrefrigerated for months.

Tibetans who live in cities have more variety in their diet. They make a steamed meat dumpling called *momo* and a noodle soup called *thukpa*. In addition, city dwellers can obtain fresh fruits and vegetables. Tibetans especially like to add onions and chillies to some of their dishes.

In Lhasa, noodles replace some traditional Tibetan food.

Although in the cities some Tibetans have started wearing Western-style clothing, most Tibetans continue to wear traditional clothes. Generally Tibetans wear subdued, neutral colors. The *chuba* is a long-sleeved jacket made of sheepskin or wool. The sleeves extend over the hands to keep them warm. The chuba is tied around the waist and is sometimes worn over one shoulder. Men, women, and children wear chubas. Today, they are worn mainly by nomads.

Women wear black or brown dresses, jumpers, skirts, and pants. Under a jumper, they might wear a light-colored blouse. Over these clothes, women wear a colorful striped apron. The wealth of a Tibetan family is put into jewelry that the women wear, usually necklaces, earrings, and hair ornaments. Tibetan women weave turquoise, coral, and silver jewels into their long braids. Many women try to have 108 braids, representing the 108 bodhisattvas.

Strands of turquoise hair ornaments adorn these Tibetan women's braids.

Tibetans love to wear hats, and each region is known for a particular style—from brocade, fur-lined hats to woolen hoods. Traditional shoes and boots are made of leather and felt from yak hair. Today, however, many Tibetans wear Western-style loafers and athletic shoes.

Housing

Traditional housing is becoming rarer in Tibet. Many of the traditional homes in cities have been pulled down, especially those that once stood near the Potala Palace in Lhasa. The area in front of the Potala is now a huge square for parades. The traditional homes are being replaced with gray concrete buildings. In an attempt to look traditional, colorful designs are painted above doorways and windows. Electricity and solar energy supply some city homes. But none have central heating.

Even the black yak-wool tents of the nomads are being replaced by houses because nomads no longer move their herds great distances. Attempts are being made to provide nomads with electric power through solar and wind energy.

Most homes in rural villages built before 1950 are in the traditional style. They were built with stone or dried-mud bricks, and have a pounded earth floor. One or more carpets may cover the floor in the living areas. A two-story house is used somewhat the same way as one in North America. The first floor has the kitchen and living area. On the second floor, everyone sleeps in one big room to keep warm. Few rural homes have electricity. Light is provided by yak-butter lamps.

Festivals and Holidays

Almost every month Tibetans can take part in a festival or celebrate a holiday. Some holidays are also holy days on which events are remembered from the Buddha's life or from the lives of important Tibetan Buddhist leaders. For example, Monlam, or the Great Prayer Festival, takes place in Lhasa in the first month of the Tibetan calendar, February or March, to celebrate the Buddha's victory over his enemies. An image of the Buddha who is still to come is carried around the outside of the Jokhang Temple. Pilgrims follow behind in procession.

In May, or in the fourth month in the Tibetan calendar, the Buddha's birth, enlightenment, and death are celebrated in the Sakadawa festival.

Tibetans celebrate in colorful costumes.

In the seventh month, August, Tibetans have fun at the Yogurt Festival and the Bathing Festival. Monks at monasteries in Lhasa and other parts of Tibet are brought yogurt to break a long period of fasting. Then the monks perform cham dances and religious dramas for the people. By August, river waters are warm enough to bathe in. Parents and children jump in the water and wash themselves and their clothing This not only washes off the old dirt but is supposed to protect them from disease in the coming year.

Tibetan horse-racing festival

Horse-racing festivals are held throughout Tibet in July and September. Besides the horse races, there is usually one funny race on yaks. Another contest is shooting at a target with a bow and arrow while riding on horseback. Other riders try to reach down and pick up a *khata* (white scarf) from the ground as they gallop by. These races celebrate Tibet's long history of horsemanship.

In the twelfth lunar month (January), the last festival of the year takes place. Again, monks perform cham dances in which the masked spirit collects all the evil that has happened during the year and throws it away. Tibetans must truly pray during this festival that the bad times they have suffered during the past fifty years will end and that they will soon gain more control over their lives.

National Holidays in Tibet

These holidays are celebrated in Tibet because it is part of the People's Republic of China.

New Year's Day	January 1
Chinese New Year	Date varies
International Working Women's Day	March 8
International Labor Day	May 1
Youth Day	May 4
Children's Day	June 1
Founding of the Communist Party of China Day	July 1
Founding of the People's Liberation Army Day	August 1
Teacher's Day	September 10
National Day	October 1

Timeline

Tibetan History

	About
People are living in Tibet.	28,000 B.C.
People are living near Lhasa.	About 18,000 B.C.
Farming begins in the Yarlung Tsangpo River valley.	About 50 B.C.–A.D. 300
Songtsen Gampo unites Tibet; Buddhism comes to Tibet; a written Tibetan language is developed.	A.D. 630–650
A treaty between China and Tibet recognizes Tibet as separate from China.	821
Atisha arrives in Tibet from India to teach about Buddhism.	1042
Rinpung princes control Tibet.	1435–1565
Tsang kings control Tibet.	1565–1642
Mongol leader gives the lama of Drepung Monastery the title of *dalai*, "ocean of wisdom."	1578
Ngawang Lobsang Gyatso, the Great Fifth Dalai Lama, brings all of Tibet under his control.	1642–1682

World History

2500 B.C.	Egyptians build the Pyramids and the Sphinx in Giza.
563 B.C.	The Buddha is born in India.
A.D. 313	The Roman emperor Constantine recognizes Christianity.
610	The Prophet Muhammad begins preaching a new religion called Islam.
1054	The Eastern (Orthodox) and Western (Roman) Churches break apart.
1066	William the Conqueror defeats the English in the Battle of Hastings.
1095	Pope Urban II proclaims the First Crusade.
1215	King John seals the Magna Carta.
1300s	The Renaissance begins in Italy.
1347	The Black Death sweeps through Europe.
1453	Ottoman Turks capture Constantinople, conquering the Byzantine Empire.
1492	Columbus arrives in North America.
1500s	The Reformation leads to the birth of Protestantism.

Tibetan History

Mongols invade Tibet.	1705
Manchus invade Tibet, drive out Mongols, and declare Tibet a protectorate of China.	1720
British troops capture Lhasa.	1903
Tibetans remove all Manchus from Tibet.	1912
Thirteenth Dalai Lama proclaims Tibet's independence.	1913
Britain recognizes Tibet's independence by agreeing on the India-Tibet border at the Simla Conference.	1914
Chinese Communists begin invading Tibet.	1950
Representatives of Tibet's government are forced to sign the Seventeen-Point Agreement; Chinese troops enter Lhasa.	1951
Tibetans stage an uprising in Lhasa; the Dalai Lama flees to India.	1959
China's Cultural Revolution comes to Tibet; monasteries are destroyed; monks and nuns are imprisoned; harsh economic measures are imposed.	1966–1976
The Dalai Lama proposes a five-point peace plan for Tibet.	1987
Chinese soldiers kill or imprison demonstrators in Lhasa; China puts Tibet under martial law.	1987–1989
Dalai Lama is awarded the Nobel Peace Prize.	1989
President George H. W. Bush becomes the first U.S. president to meet with the Dalai Lama.	1991
Senior lamas name a new Panchen Lama; Chinese kidnap him and his parents and name a different Panchen Lama.	1995
Leader of the Karmapa order flees to India.	2000
President George W. Bush meets with Chinese leaders in both Beijing and Washington and urges restoring Tibetans' human rights.	2002

World History

1776	The Declaration of Independence is signed.
1789	The French Revolution begins.
1865	The American Civil War ends.
1914	World War I breaks out.
1917	The Bolshevik Revolution brings communism to Russia.
1929	Worldwide economic depression begins.
1939	World War II begins, following the German invasion of Poland.
1945	World War II ends.
1957	The Vietnam War starts.
1969	Humans land on the moon.
1975	The Vietnam War ends.
1979	Soviet Union invades Afghanistan.
1983	Drought and famine in Africa.
1989	The Berlin Wall is torn down, as communism crumbles in Eastern Europe.
1991	Soviet Union breaks into separate states.
1992	Bill Clinton is elected U.S. president.
2000	George W. Bush is elected U.S. president.
2001	Terrorists attack World Trade Towers, New York and the Pentagon, Washington, D.C.

Fast Facts

Official name: Tibet Autonomous Region of the People's Republic of China

Capital: Lhasa

Official languages: Chinese, Tibetan

City of Shigatse

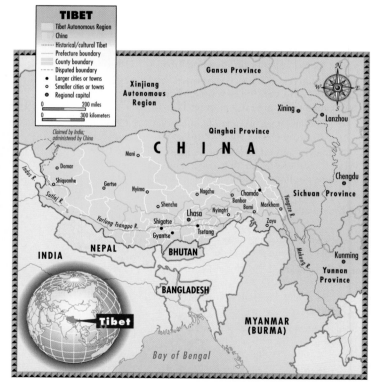

China's flag

Mount Everest

Official religion:	None
Year of founding:	1965
National anthem:	"March of the Volunteers" (People's Republic of China)
Government:	One-party regional government with one legislative house
Chief political leader:	Secretary of the Communist Party of China in Tibet
Area and dimensions:	471,662 square miles (1,221,600 sq km)
Greatest distance north to south:	620 miles (998 km)
Greatest distance east to west:	2,030 miles (3,267 km)
Coordinates of geographic center:	32° North latitude, 88° East longitude
Bordering countries:	Regions and provinces of the People's Republic of China to the north and east; Myanmar (Burma) to the southeast; India, Nepal, and Bhutan to the south; India to the west.
Highest elevation:	Mount Everest (*Chomolungma*), 29,035 feet (8,850 m) above sea level
Lowest elevation:	5,297 feet (1,615 m) above sea level on the big bend of the Yarlung Tsangpo River
Average temperatures:	Highest: 58°F (14°C); lowest: 24°F (−4°C)
Average annual precipitation:	Highest: 78 inches (198 cm) in the southeast; lowest: less than 2 inches (5 cm) in the north

Yumbu Lagang Palace

**TAR population
(2001 est.):** 2,620,000

**Population of
largest cities:**

Lhasa	200,000
Shigatse	60,000
Tsetang	25,000
Gyantse	15,000

Famous landmarks:
- ▶ *Chang Tang Nature Reserve*, northern Tibet
- ▶ *Drepung* and *Sera Monasteries*, Lhasa
- ▶ *Jokhang Temple*, Lhasa
- ▶ *Kumbum Chorten*, Gyantse
- ▶ *Mapham Tso (Lake Manasarovarr)*, in western Tibet
- ▶ *Mount Everest*, on border with Nepal
- ▶ *Mount Kailash*, western Tibet
- ▶ *Nam Tso*, a lake on the Chang Tang Plateau
- ▶ *Potala Palace*, Lhasa
- ▶ *Yamdrok Tso*, a lake near Lhasa
- ▶ *Yumbu Lagang Palace*, Tsetang

Currency

Industry: Tibet's major industries are the manufacture of cement, salt, vegetable oil, textiles, leather goods, and beer. Traditional handicrafts account for more than 2,000 products including hand-knotted carpets; woolen fabric; wooden bowls; gold and silver jewelry; and special Tibetan aprons, quilts, shoes, and hats. Chromite, tinkalite, lithium, and boromagnesite are leading mining products. Lumbering and logging are important in southeast TAR

Currency: The *yuan* (Y). March 2003 exchange rate: U.S.$1 = 8.28Y

A young monk

Tenzin Gyatso, the Dalai Lama

Weights and measures:	Metric system for international dealings; Chinese system within Tibet: 1 *chi* = 1.09 feet (0.33 m); 1 *mu* = 0.16 acre (0.06 ha); 1 *jin* = 1.10 pounds (0.5 kg)	
Literacy rate:	44 percent	
Common Tibetan words and phrases:	*Kale phe.* (kah-leh phe)	Good-bye.
	Kay-nang-gi-ma-ray. (keh-nang-gi-mah-rey)	You're welcome.
	Kayrang gusu debo yimbay? (keh-rahng ku-su de-bo yin-peh)	How are you?
	Kayrang gi mingla karay sa? (keh-rahng gi ming-la kay-rey yin)	What is your name?
	Kayrang lung-pa ka-ne yin? (keh-rahng loong-ba kah-nay yin)	Where are you from?
	Kyok-tsenanda. (kie-owk seh-ahn-da)	Excuse me.
	Tashi dele. (ta-shi de-leg)	Hello.
	Tujaychay. (thu-je-che)	Thank you.

Famous Tibetans:

Songtsen Gampo
Yarlung king   (608–650)

Ngawang Lobsang Gyatso
Great Fifth Dalai Lama   (1617–1682)

Tenzin Gyatso
Fourteenth Dalai Lama, Nobel Peace Prize winner   (1935–)

Milarepa
Poet-monk   (1040–1123)

Thonmi Sambhota
Developed Tibetan alphabet and writing system   (seventh century)

To Find Out More

Books

▶ Booz, Elisabeth B. *Tibet: Roof of the World*. Lincolnwood, Ill.: Passport Books, 1994.

▶ Dolphin, Laurie. *Our Journey from Tibet: Based on a True Story*. New York: Dutton Children's Books, 1997.

▶ Hyde-Chambers, Fredrick, and Audrey Hyde-Chambers. *Tibetan Folk Tales*. Boulder, Co.: Shambhala, 1995.

▶ Kendra, Judith. *Tibetans*. Threatened Cultures. New York: Thomson Learning, 1994.

▶ Kizilos, Peter. *Tibet: Disputed Land*. World in Conflict. Minneapolis: Lerner Publications, 2000.

▶ Levy, Patricia. *Tibet*. Cultures of the World. Tarrytown, N.Y.: Marshall Cavendish, 1996.

▶ Lukas, Sarah K., Kitty Leaken, and Clare Harris. *The Art of Exile: Paintings by Tibetan Children in India*. Santa Fe: Museum of New Mexico Press, 1997.

▶ Sís, Peter. *Tibet through the Red Box*. New York: Farrar Straus Giroux, 1998.

▶ *Tibet: A Portrait of the Country through Its Festivals and Traditions*. Danbury, Conn.: Grolier Educational, 1999.

▶ Whitesel, Cheryl Aylward. *Rebel: A Tibetan Odyssey*. New York: Harper Collins, 2000.

Video Recordings

▶ *Tibet: On the Edge of Change*. William Bacon Production, Questor Video Collection, Questor Inc., 1998.

▶ *Tibet: The End of Time*. Time-Life's Lost Civilizations. Alexandria, Va.: Time-Life Video and Television, 1995.

Web Sites

▶ **China Tibet Information Center**
http://www.tibetinfor.com
Site presents Chinese view of Tibet through daily newspaper articles with links to Chinese newspapers and news agencies, as well as pages on the economy, culture, and daily life in Tibet.

▶ **The Government of Tibet in Exile**
http://www.tibet.com
Site managed by the Office of Tibet, the official agency of the Dalai Lama; includes news articles and links to information on the status, government, and culture of Tibet.

▶ **International Campaign for Tibet**
http://www.savetibet.org
Official site of the International Campaign for Tibet, which works to promote human rights and self-determination for Tibetans; includes news articles, an explanation of Tibet's status, and ways to help the cause.

▶ **Tibet Daily**
http://tibetpost.com
Neutral news site with an up-to-date daily listing of news articles with links to many other sites on Tibet.

▶ **Tibetan Plateau Project**
http://www.earthisland.org/tpp/
Site devoted to conservation of natural environment of the Tibetan Plateau, with special pages on its programs to protect endangered species.

Organizations and Embassies

▶ **International Campaign for Tibet, U.S. Tibet Committee**
1518 K Street NW, Suite 410
Washington, DC 20005-1401
202-785-1515

▶ **Jacques Marchais Center of Tibetan Art**
338 Lighthouse Avenue
Staten Island, NY 10306
212-987-3478

▶ **Office of Tibet**
241 East 32nd Street
New York, NY 10016
212-213-5010

▶ **Tibetan Cultural Center**
3655 South Snoddy Road
Bloomington, IN 47401
812-334-7046

▶ **Tibet House**
22 West 15th Street
New York, NY 10003
212-807-0563

Index

Page numbers in *italics* indicate illustrations.

Meet the Author

Patricia K. Kummer writes and edits textbook materials and nonfiction books for children and young adults from her home office in Lisle, Illinois. She earned a bachelor of arts degree in history from the College of St. Catherine in St. Paul, Minnesota, and a master of arts degree in history from Marquette University in Milwaukee, Wisconsin. Before starting her career in publishing, she taught social studies at the junior high/middle-school level.

Since then, she has written about U.S., African, Asian, and European history for textbook publishers and "A Guide to Writing and Speaking" in World Book's *Word Power Library*. More recently, she wrote *Côte d'Ivoire*, *Ukraine*, and *Singapore* in the Children's Press series Enchantment of the World. *Côte d'Ivoire* won an award from Chicago Women in Publishing. One of her favorite projects was writing a commissioned biography for Jerry Reinsdorf, chairman of the Chicago Bulls and Chicago White Sox. The biography commemorates the life of his administrative assistant who died leaving a three-year-old daughter. The book was based totally on interviews. It will be presented to the daughter when she is about thirteen years old.

"Writing books about people, states, and countries requires a great deal of research," she says. "To me, researching is the most fun part of a project. For this book, I started by going online, where I found several good Web sites. I clicked on amazon.com to compile a list of the most recent books on Tibet. From there I went to the library. For the books my library didn't have, I placed interlibrary loan requests. To keep up with events in Tibet, I checked Web sites that had daily news reports on Tibet.

"However, because the Tibet Autonomous Region is not a country, I wasn't able to use many of the usual sources. That Tibet is part of a Communist country and that its status is so controversial also made it more difficult to find objective, unbiased information. Staff at the Chinese Embassy in Washington, D.C., however, tried to be helpful."

Ms. Kummer hopes that this book will help young people better understand Tibet's position in the world.

Photo Credits